Treasures of the Museum

Treasures of the Museum
Victoria, Australia

Museum Victoria, Melbourne

Published by Museum Victoria, 2004
© Text copyright Museum Victoria, 2004
© Images copyright Museum Victoria unless otherwise noted

We have made every effort to obtain copyright and moral permission for use of all material. Please advise us of any errors or omissions.

Museum Victoria
GPO Box 666E
Melbourne
Victoria 3001
Australia
(61 3) 8341 7777
www.museum.vic.gov.au

Publishers: Tim Rolfe, Melanie Raymond and Hilary Ericksen
Designers: Luisa Laino, Dot Georgoulas and Gina Batzakis
Image and copyright managers: Edwina Circuitt, Ingrid Unger and Marion Huxley
Digital production officers: Peter Bubulya and Sally Rogers-Davidson
Editor: Bryony Cosgrove

National Library of Australia Cataloguing-in-Publication Data:

Museum Victoria.
   Treasures of the Museum, Victoria, Australia.
   Includes index.
   ISBN 0 9577471 5 2.

   1. Museum Victoria – Pictorial works.
   2. Museums – Victoria – Melbourne.
   I. Title.

708.99451

Museums Board of Victoria:
Harold Mitchell, AO, President
Peter McMullin, Deputy President
Professor Diane Alcorn
Terry Garwood
Susan Heron
Peter Hiscock, AM
Dr Gael Jennings
The Hon. Joan Kirner, AM
Professor Janet McCalman
Sheila O'Sullivan
Bob Weis

Executive Management Team:
Dr J. Patrick Greene, Chief Executive Officer
Gaye Hamilton, Director, Museum Operations
Dr Robin Hirst, Director, Collections, Research and Exhibitions
Tim Hart, Director, Information, Multimedia and Technology
Joe Corponi, Director, Corporate Services

Page ii–iii: The National Museum is relocated from the University of Melbourne to its Swanston Street site
Museum Victoria Collection

Governor of Victoria's foreword

It was 1835 when John Batman stood on the banks of the Yarra River and claimed the site would be a splendid place for a village. Soon after, the township of Melbourne was growing on the traditional lands of the Wurundjeri people. By the 1850s, gold, that most coveted of all treasures, was found in Victoria. Gold shaped the changing fortunes of Melbourne and the Colony of Victoria, attracting thousands of migrants, who brought with them their aspirations for a good life as well as their cultural traditions.

The National Museum of Victoria was part of the vision of the early colonial administrators. It was established for, in the idiom of the period, the 'moral benefit' of Victorians, and its collections were associated with the colony's economic advancement.

Some 150 years later, the museum remains a cornerstone of Victoria's public life. An eminent heritage and research institution, it houses our prized natural and cultural heritage collections and it supports the state's research and development profile. The magnificent new museum building in the Carlton Gardens underscores the immense value of the museum and its work to the state.

Internationally the museum is equally important. Its collection of Aboriginal shields from south-eastern Australia, for example, is not only outstanding but is renowned worldwide among scholars working in the area. Likewise the natural history collection holds specimens that do not exist in any other museum collections and is thus of global significance. The natural history collection has many 'type' specimens, and for this factor alone it is simply priceless.

Yet the museum is always a place for the people. It touches the lives of individuals in very real ways, and often does so over many years. My own memories go back to the 1930s when, as a child, I eagerly awaited my annual visit to the museum with my grandmother. We would spend much of a whole day there. I particularly remember the model of what was at the time the world's largest gold nugget, the 'Welcome Stranger', as well as the wonderful display of jewel-like hummingbirds and the collection of machinery. My connection with the museum has continued into my adult life and, with my interest in entomology, I have spent many hours in the museum's basement, marvelling over moths, butterflies and other specimens.

The museum is a different place than it was during the visits of my childhood – like all institutions and ideas it has had to change with the times to remain relevant. The ideals of the museum, nevertheless, have endured and it continues to inform the private, public and professional lives of Victorians.

It is both a place for our state treasures and a place to be treasured.

John Landy, AC, MBE
Governor of Victoria

Chief Executive Officer's foreword

How can it be possible to select just a handful of treasures from a vast collection to represent a century and a half of collecting by the museum? That is the task the contributors to this book were set. What emerges is an eclectic mix of items, with learned descriptions and, in the case of several objects, personal reminiscences from guest contributors. Numerous entries relate to groups of objects. These include five surgical instruments used by Sir Edward 'Weary' Dunlop, pearl-shell ornaments made by Aboriginal people in Central Australia and a selection of objects found in the excavations at Little Lonsdale Street in Melbourne. What matters in making such a selection is the way in it represents the richness of the collection and the heritage of all Australians, indeed of humanity more generally.

Surgical instruments, pearl shells and broken pottery do not, in themselves, constitute valuable objects, but they are treasures because of their association with, respectively, a remarkable Australian, Indigenous people of Central Australia and the inhabitants of 19th-century inner-city Melbourne. Museum objects are like comets travelling through time and space, trailing streams of meanings. The skill of the museum is to make those meanings apparent and available. The museum has its own 'treasures' who make that possible: members of staff, volunteers and associates who collect, research, conserve, display, teach, present, interpret and carry out all the other functions necessary to make a great international institution function smoothly. The labour of generations of staff in building, caring for and interpreting our collection is what gives the museum its high standing among museums worldwide.

Museums cannot exist without a broad range of support in the communities they serve. The decision by the Victorian Legislative Council in September 1853 to provide public funds for the establishment of a museum was remarkably far-sighted. Melbourne had been settled for only 18 years, and the Colony of Victoria was just two years old. Successive governments have supported the museum as it has developed and evolved. Many private individuals, foundations, companies and agencies have donated collections and made grants. In a book of treasures, their precious support should also be acknowledged.

The entries in this volume will whet the appetite of the reader. If so much fascinating information can be presented about this small selection from such a vast collection, what other riches exist? Everyone has an opportunity to make their own journey of discovery in our three museums, as well as the Royal Exhibition Building. We hope that every exploration proves to be an experience to be treasured.

Dr J. Patrick Greene
Chief Executive Officer

The Lyrebird-habitat display at the National Museum of Victoria, 1906
Museum Victoria Collection

Contents

Governor of Victoria's foreword	v
Chief Executive Officer's foreword	vii
Introduction	1
Australian Society and Technology	8
Indigenous Cultures	76
Sciences	140
Notes on contributors	202
Acknowledgments	204
Photography credits	204
Index	205

The gorilla case sits centre-stage at the museum's University of Melbourne location, c. 1870
Source: La Trobe Picture Collection, State Library of Victoria

Phar Lap, Australia's most famous racehorse

Introduction

Any publication about the treasures of the Museum Victoria Collection has to include the animal registered 'C 10726'. That number in the mammalogy database refers to Phar Lap. Of all the 16 million items that the museum holds, none has the popular appeal of Big Red, the Mighty Conqueror. The museum has irreplaceable scientific specimens and unique artefacts of cultural and historical significance, studied and revered by scholars across the world, but the question visitors ask more than any other is, 'Where's Phar Lap?'

The chestnut racehorse is one of Australia's most popular sporting champions and the subject of legend, having won 37 of his 51 races between 1928 and 1932, before an untimely death during an ill-fated venture to the United States. Today, Phar Lap stands proudly in the Australia Gallery. The surrounding walls are cloaked in his carmine, black and white racing colours. It is a remarkable experience to visit Phar Lap and watch the different generations walk slowly around him, look up and speak in whispers, as if paying homage in a sacred space. The people have made sure Phar Lap's spirit endures. The people have made Phar Lap a treasure.

Apart from popular appeal, what makes a museum treasure? Every few years, the museum employs official valuers to estimate the worth of the whole collection. The total figure runs into hundreds of millions of dollars. As a result of this exercise, we have a list of the objects and specimens with the highest valuations. In compiling *Treasures of the Museum*, we could have simply put together a book based around this list. For the people who assemble, research and care for the collection, however, a treasure comprises much more than its dollar value.

Curators, collection managers, other colleagues and friends were asked to make their own choices. The treasures featured include popular icons and rare and unique items, important cultural artefacts, technological innovations and achievements, and critical pieces of scientific evidence. They represent major historical milestones and highlights of human achievement, and simply the weird and the wonderful. Above all, each object is treasured. From Phar Lap to fencing wire, from the Giant Gippsland Earthworm to gold nuggets, from CSIRAC to sharks, from the Tasmanian Tiger to Tjeby, each object has a well-earned place on this list of our most meaningful heritage.

Distinguished by a magnificent and diverse range of material, this book is structured into three sections: Australian Society and Technology, Indigenous Cultures, and Sciences. These sections reflect the museum's key collecting areas. Each page recounts the unique story of the treasure (or treasures) featured, together with images of each. These individual stories give the selection meaning and significance. The stories are recounted by museum staff and by guest writers, each of whom has a particular relationship with the object (or objects) about which they write. *Treasures of the Museum*, however, can provide only a glimpse of the museum's substantial collection. The book presents moments in the museum's history rather than a comprehensive overview. For this, Carolyn Rasmussen's *A Museum for the People: A History of Museum Victoria and its Predecessors, 1854–2000*, published in 2001, is the perfect companion piece.

Some museum objects are important because of their associations with particular people, places or times. We need to take into consideration the circumstances of an object's acquisition, and to look at additional details to assess its true significance. For instance, among the material collected by renowned anthropologist Donald Thomson, there is an unassuming wooden spearthrower acquired from a Pintupi man in the Western Desert in

Walter Baldwin Spencer, director of the National Museum of Victoria from 1899 to 1928
Source: Dr Kingsley Rowan

Frederick McCoy, director of the National Museum of Victoria from 1858 to 1899
Source: La Trobe Picture Collection, State Library of Victoria

1957. The spearthrower is decorated simply with a series of 36 concentric circles and interconnecting lines. But the piece takes on new meaning after a study of Thomson's field notes and photographs from that time. The design is actually a map of the 36 waterholes of the area – essential knowledge in order to survive in that country. This spearthrower is part of a landmark collection of cultural artefacts, natural history specimens, field notes and audiovisual material collected by Thomson and which the museum now looks after.

Like Donald Thomson, a number of prominent figures in the history of the museum worked across various scientific or cultural disciplines, and amassed a treasure trove for the institution over the years. Professor (later Sir) Walter Baldwin Spencer was the National Museum director from 1899 to 1928. He was primarily a biologist, but also pursued an interest in anthropology and carried out major expeditions to study Aboriginal communities in Central and northern Australia. He built up a precious collection of Indigenous artefacts, along with supporting notes and photography, and motion picture and sound recordings. This material was the basis for his seminal work *The Native Tribes of Central Australia*, and the interrelationships of many of the objects are still the subject of investigation and interpretation.

Similarly, Professor (later Sir) Frederick McCoy, director of the National Museum from 1858 to 1899, sourced material both locally and overseas to help establish the priceless natural history collection at the museum. This led to his encyclopaedic works *Prodromus of the Zoology of Victoria* and *Prodromus of the Palaeontology of Victoria*, which described the animal species found in the state. It was an ambitious and wide-ranging program. McCoy achieved remarkable coverage of Victoria's living

Introduction

Aboriginal material on display in the Spencer Gallery, National Musem of Victoria, c. 1939
Source: Private collection

and extinct fauna, and his systematic collection forms an important basis for the museum's natural history holdings. The collection continues to be highly valued as a record of species occurring in Victoria in the late 19th century.

The museum has its origins in the Museum of Natural History, which opened on 9 March 1854 and was housed in the Government Assay Office in La Trobe Street, Melbourne. At that stage, Victoria, an independent colony since 1851, was experiencing a boom brought about by the gold rushes. The local regions of Melbourne and Geelong were occupied by a population of more than 80 000 people and nearly 6 million sheep. As the surrounding countryside was explored, the first collections of new and unusual geological and biological specimens began to take shape.

The collection was transferred to more distinguished surroundings at the University of Melbourne in Parkville in 1856, and the museum quickly burgeoned and became formally known as the National Museum of Victoria. New items made their way into the collection as mining and agricultural industries grew rapidly in Victoria during the latter half of the 19th century. The museum benefited from a wealth of local as well as international acquisitions. In 1899, the museum was uprooted again and relocated in the Public Library building in Swanston Street, where it was to remain for the next 100 years.

The National Museum of Victoria's collections continued to grow steadily, and in addition to accommodating the natural sciences, the institution soon took on collecting in anthropology in the early 1900s (ethnology had previously come under the auspices of the Public Library and the Industrial and Technological Museum). The practices of purchase and donation were supplemented by a program of museum expeditions and fieldwork within Victoria and interstate. Over the years, important material from the geological, biological and ethnographic collections was exhibited in the various museum galleries, including the grand McCoy Hall.

The other predecessor of Museum Victoria was the Industrial and Technological Museum, which originally opened in the Public Library building in Swanston Street

Skeleton of a whale found at Jan Juc beach, assembled outside the museum at its University of Melbourne location, 1868
Museum Victoria Collection

Introduction

in 1870, and then developed in parallel with the National Museum for more than a century. Its foundation was a collection of mining and agricultural exhibits brought to Melbourne for the Intercolonial Exhibition of 1866. The Industrial and Technological Museum eventually became the Science Museum of Victoria.

A pivotal year for the museum was 1983, when Melbourne's two big museums on the Swanston Street site, the National Museum of Victoria and the Science Museum of Victoria, amalgamated to form the Museum of Victoria. For the first time, the state's natural history, technology and human history collections were managed in an integrated way, and under the one roof. While many of the collection highlights were displayed in the exhibition galleries and halls, much of the research and reference material was kept out of sight in a labyrinth of brick-lined tunnels under McCoy Hall. Affectionately known as 'the dungeons', these areas were occasionally opened to the public; 'dungeon tours' always drew large crowds, with intrigued visitors queuing around the block.

Several new museum facilities were commissioned and completed during the 1990s. Scienceworks at Spotswood was opened in 1992, featuring the science and technology collections, and the Immigration Museum in Flinders Street opened in 1998. In 2000, the flagship of Museum Victoria opened alongside the Royal Exhibition Building in Carlton Gardens, exhibiting thousands of objects from many discipline areas.

Museum Victoria as we know it today has grown to a large and diverse organisation. Historically, it has always had a primary role as the Victorian state museum, collecting the state's natural and cultural heritage. It also continues to develop and manage a collection of great significance, utilising the talents of over 80 curatorial and collection management staff.

One of the privileges of working at the museum is the opportunity to interact with the collection on a daily basis. A curator or collection manager, with responsibility for a specific part of the cultural or scientific collection, develops an intimate knowledge of the museum's material. That specialist knowledge contributes to a huge database of information about the collection, built up by generations of workers since the institution's establishment. Some curators have worked at the museum for over 30 years, building and enhancing the collection day by day. But in an organisation with such a long and continuing history, staff members are simply custodians. Eventually, they will hand over the task of stewardship to the next generation, and the collection and the knowledge that makes it meaningful will continue to grow and be safeguarded for generations to come.

With the rapid development of the museum over the last 20 years, there have been major improvements in storage facilities for the collection. Previous perceptions of museums might have been of grimy and dusty specimens, reeking of mothballs and packed to the rafters in dark and musty vaults. This is a far cry from what we see today. With an extensive and valuable collection built up over many decades, the museum does not take its responsibilities lightly. Storage facilities are world class and built to meet strict collection management and conservation standards. Environmental controls in each store mean that material is kept at the proper temperature, humidity and light levels. Archival-quality storage cabinets and shelving mean that objects and specimens are kept in a clean, safe environment to help ensure their survival. Our treasures are cared for both in and out of the public's gaze.

With such a vast and fragile collection, and a limited amount of exhibition space, we can have only a small percentage of the collection on public display at any one time. Robust items are suitable for permanent exhibition, while others are more fragile and can be on display for only a few months at a time. Some objects are so susceptible to light damage that they can be exhibited only briefly. Others make special appearances on occasions such as the 'Out of the Vaults' days, or can be inspected during behind-the-scenes collection tours.

Many of the museum's buildings are architectural treasures in their own right. The museum in Carlton Gardens, an award-winning creation by architects Denton Corker Marshall, is a colourful assemblage of buildings anchored within a 'super-grid' and flanked by enormous raked canopies. It sits in stark contrast to the Royal Exhibition Building with its domed Great Hall, designed by Joseph Reed for the 1880–81 Melbourne International Exhibition. Together these two important buildings form the centrepiece of the historic gardens. In the city centre, the Immigration Museum is housed in the classical Old Customs House, dating from 1876 and designed by John James Clark. In the west, the Scienceworks complex includes the historic 19th-century Spotswood Pumping Station, the plans of which are attributed to Christian Kussmaul. This distinguished set of buildings comprises significant cultural heritage, which we manage with a similar level of care to that of our collection.

The museum is always looking to acquire new material. Acquisition is not a random process but is guided by a sound collection policy and expert advice from curators. Sometimes there is an element of luck, and we know straight away that we have obtained a valuable item. Recently, the museum acquired racetrack photographs of Phar Lap after a chance encounter with the donor via the museum's website. At other times, it might take years for the true value of a treasure to become apparent, such as the discovery of a new crustacean species from among marine invertebrate collections that have been at the museum for 50 years. In yet other areas we are creating new collections, such as a tissue bank

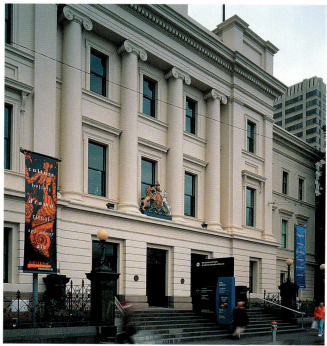

1 Museum Victoria's newest venue sits alongside the historic Royal Exhibition Building in Carlton Gardens
2 The Immigration Museum in Old Customs House, Flinders Street
Photographer: Ben Wrigley
3 The Royal Exhibition Building, of which Museum Victoria is the custodian
4 Scienceworks and the Spotswood Pumping Station in Melbourne's west
Photographer: David Loram, DDL Photographics

Introduction

3

4

representing Australian fauna, which will be used in DNA and molecular studies in order to better understand evolutionary relationships.

It is hard to be definitive about the material we will acquire in the future, but there are some definite themes we will explore as we try to monitor a rapidly changing world: Indigenous relationships and reconciliation, immigration and cultural diversity, our place in the Pacific and South-East Asia, the natural environment, sustainability and technological change. The museum's current research strategy is focused in the areas of society and technology, sciences and Indigenous cultures. And while curatorial staff carry out research on the collection, we also invite postgraduate students and researchers from other parts of Australia and throughout the world to study the collection and add to our knowledge.

The museum's partnership with Indigenous communities, and our involvement in the repatriation process, is an important case in point. We work with Aboriginal traditional custodians to identify material that in some cases has been held in the collection for more than 100 years. Indigenous people have been able to give vital additional perspectives to a large portion of the collection. These efforts sometimes uncover Aboriginal human remains and secret sacred material, which were probably acquired in good faith by people at the time, but are no longer appropriate for the museum to keep. In accordance with the museum's repatriation policy, we continue to work with Indigenous communities to return this material to the traditional owners. This is indicative of a tremendous shift in museum attitudes and sensibilities, and our commitment to reaching out and engaging with various communities.

To visit Museum Victoria is to experience the real thing: the authentic objects and specimens that comprise our cultural and natural history. This heritage allows us a special view of the world in which we live.

Robin Hirst and Timothy Stranks

Detail of the showman's steam traction engine model (see page 17)

Australian Society and Technology

Treasures of the Museum

Indian arms

When mutiny broke out in India in 1857 it sent shock waves through the British Empire. For over a century, India had been considered the great success of British colonisation. Recognising that the mutineers' captured weapons probably would be destroyed, the chairman of the Public Library's trustees, Redmond Barry, wrote to Governor Barkly suggesting that Barkly exert his influence to secure some of them. In Victoria, Barry argued, the weapons, 'would be highly prized; such objects placed in the Museum attached to the Library would afford interesting illustration of oriental national customs and peculiarities'. The collection of 287 items, described in an accompanying letter as 'of value and rarity', arrived in November 1860 and was displayed in the library's main stairwell. The weapons were subsequently transferred to the museum. BT

Savage Model 1907 pistol

In 1959, the museum received a superbly engraved American Savage Model 1907 automatic pistol. The Victorian Police had confiscated it from its owner, but believing the pistol might be of some historical significance, presented it to the museum. The blue metal frame is engraved with an oak-leaf vine motif. The mother-of-pearl grips are inlaid with a golden medallion bearing the Savage logo of an Indian chief. The pistol is stamped with the serial number '1'. The initials 'BA' (now appearing as 'PA' due to a missing portion of the inlay) are inlaid in gold on the barrel. The pistol's high quality and distinctive markings suggest it originally belonged to the president of the Savage Arms Company, Colonel Benjamin Adriance. BT

1 Flintlock blunderbuss (early 19th century), European origin, L 57 cm

2 Indian matchlock musket (early 19th century), L 155.5 cm

3 Savage Model 1907, .32 calibre automatic pistol (1908), Savage Arms Co., L 16.7 cm

Australian Society and Technology

Colonial artefacts of the Victorian Navy

Before Federation, Victoria boasted its own colonial navy. The Victorian Navy was formed in the 1850s, when the Crimean War and regular shipments of gold bullion from the goldfields created a fear that Melbourne might be attacked by sea. Victoria's first warship, the steam sloop *Victoria*, was launched in England on 30 June 1855. The sloop was joined by the *Nelson*, a veteran, wooden-hulled Royal Navy battleship of 1814, and the *Cerberus*, one of the world's first armour-plated, ironclad battleships with turret-mounted guns.

The museum holds a small but significant collection of artefacts relating to both the technological and social history of the colonial navy. Among these are two Nordenfelt quick-firing, five-barrel, .45-inch calibre guns, representing a new type of armament introduced to counter the threat posed by torpedoes. The Nordenfelt, manufactured in the United Kingdom, is an early form of machine gun, configured to fire each barrel either in rapid succession or in combined volleys. Four 1-inch calibre Nordenfelt guns were first fitted to the *Cerberus* in 1879, while the examples held by the museum are thought to have been fitted to smaller torpedo launches around 1887.

This engraved brass snuffbox, of unusual shape, was designed to fit snugly in a waistcoat pocket. It was owned originally by Joseph Ovenden, who served on the *Victoria* during the first New Zealand Maori War of 1860 and who was later chief bosun's mate on the *Nelson*. Snuff-taking was popular among sailors in the colonial navy; sailors were prohibited from smoking onboard ship for fear of causing an accidental gunpowder explosion. MC

Nordenfelt five-barrel, .45-inch calibre quick-firing gun (c. 1887), Nordenfelt Gun & Ammunition Co. Ltd, H 66 x W 66 x L 134 cm
Pocket snuffbox (c. 1860), unknown make, H 3 x W 4.5 x L 8 cm

Treasures of the Museum

Honour certificate

The museum holds uniforms, guns, photographs, diaries, artworks and printed material from the First World War. This artwork, designed for use as a domestic memorial, depicts the nation's respect and gratitude for those who fought and returned.

During the First World War, Cecil Smith was employed as a graphic artist by D.W. Paterson and Company, a well-established printing firm in Collins Street, Melbourne. Smith designed a number of honour certificates for presentation by local authorities to returning war veterans, to thank them for their service and to welcome them home. The museum holds four of his designs, including those for the City of Footscray and for the Shepparton Town Council.

Earlier honour certificates had portrayed Australian soldiers in battle, emphasising their bravery and the hardships they had suffered. Sometimes the certificates acted as spurs to encourage further enlistment. This design, however, was finished at the end of 1917, after Australian forces had suffered huge losses in the war. Its mood is different – quieter and more solemn – and it depicts a nation's gratitude for the sacrifices of its volunteers.

The young woman, representing Australia, kneels in homage, offering laurel, a symbol of victory, to the returned veteran. The soldier's tin hat and rifle lie abandoned, but a flame burns eternally in memory of his service. The names of the allied nations remind the recipient and his family that his contribution was part of an international war effort. Great Britain is represented by roses, thistles and clover at the base of the design. EW

Cecil G. Smith, First World War honour certificate (c. 1917), H 51 x W 35.4 cm

Australian Society and Technology

Orrery

An orrery is a mechanical model of the solar system. The first orrery was made around 1713 and is generally attributed to watchmaker George Graham. A copy of Graham's machine was made for Charles Boyle, the Fourth Earl of Orrery, who gave his name to the model.

The 18th and 19th centuries were a time of renewed interest in automata, reflecting the idea that mechanical science could unlock the secrets of nature. Mechanisms of this period included flute players, singing birds and even a lawyer arguing in court.

Orreries were popular educational devices, yet they are inaccurate representations of the solar system. Most orreries correctly represent the relative speeds of different planets, but few accurately show the relative sizes of the planets and their planetary orbits, or the elliptical shape of the orbits.

This orrery, manufactured by Benjamin Martin in 1770, contains a mechanism that can produce elliptical orbits. It also differs from earlier orreries by having the planets on extended arms, rather than fixed on rotating plates. Martin was one of the most important instrument makers of his time and was particularly known for his microscopes. MB

Benjamin Martin, orrery (1770), H 38.5 x diam. 25.5 cm

Treasures of the Museum

Max Mints toys

Around 1929, former milliner Johanna Hillier began moulding hundreds of delicate waxed paper wrappers from MacRobertson's Max Mints into an astonishing array of toys for her three grandchildren.

Mrs Hillier's grand-daughter Ruth received a set of over 50 of these toys. She brought them out on rainy Sunday afternoons and always laid them on a white cloth, handling them with special care. Except for a few, such as the Noah's Ark, most of the toys related to 'playing house'.

Ruth's set contained everything necessary to kit out an elaborate doll's house. Furnishings included a bed, a wardrobe full of clothes, tables, lamps, a chaise longue and even a carpet. Small touches such as candlestick holders and serviette rings, and work tools such as brooms and a washing line enhanced the sense of domestic authenticity. The set also included a range of doll's costumes and accessories – the brightly coloured and patterned wrappers were perfect for dresses, hats, handbags and fans.

More than simply a child's play things, these unique artefacts are an innovative example of domestic craft. They tell the story of a grandmother's devotion and creativity in an era when resourcefulness was prized. In 1989, Ruth donated her Max Mints toys to the museum, where they delight new generations. FK

Noah's Ark, complete with carved wooden animals (1929–35), H 11 x W 8 x L 23 cm

A doll's wardrobe with clothes and accessories (1929–35), wardrobe H 16 x W 7.8 cm

Australian Society and Technology

The Australian Children's Folklore Collection

'Ink pink, you stink!' Girl, age 6, Myrtleford, 1977.
Pad and pencil, tape recorder and camera were the tools with which field researchers June Factor and Gwenda Davey armed themselves during the 1970s and 1980s in order to document Australian children's play. We can collect a set of marbles or a length of string, but that will not record how to 'shoot a Tom Bowler' or create a 'cat's cradle'. Children still chant 'Roses are red, violets are blue' but not 'Captain Cook chased a chook'. Sometimes objects are not enough to preserve the continuity and change of the lore of the playground.

The Australian Children's Folklore Collection documents verbal folkloric traditions from the 1870s to the present. This includes more than 10 000 card files recording children's games, rhymes, riddles, jokes, superstitions, taunts and chants; more than 300 traditional and homemade play artefacts; photographs and audiovisual material; and field and research studies. It is one of the largest and most significant archives of its kind in the world, reflecting Australia's cultural and regional diversity.

A unique aspect of the collection is the Australian archive of pioneering American scholar, educator and ethnographer Dr Dorothy Howard. From 1954 to 1955, Howard travelled across Australia, collecting and documenting children's games and verbal lore in cities, country towns and small rural communities. It was the first large-scale attempt to collect, analyse and discuss our children's lore and language, and it laid the foundations for research into children's folklore in this country. The Australian Children's Folklore Collection brings to the museum a direct and personal voice from children at play. MMcF

Dorothy Howard documents children's play, 1954–55
Museum Victoria Collection
Slingshot (1980s) and file cards (1960s–80s)
Knucklebones (1950s) and autograph album (1930s)

Carousel model (c. 1970s), H 60 x diam. 85 cm

Australian Society and Technology

Carousel and steam traction engine models

Alfred Mervyn Smith built working models all his life. Born in Newport, England, in 1904, Alfred trained as an electrician and worked on flying boats in Scotland during the Second World War. In 1953, he and his wife migrated to Australia. The seven models in the museum's collection were made following his retirement in the early 1970s.

Alfred loved old English carousels and created his own model with great care and attention to detail. He scavenged whatever he could find around the house for materials, including old coffee tins, pictures from magazines and cigarette packets, icy-pole sticks, pieces from board games – even his wife's jewellery. His steam traction engine replicated those used to haul amusement rides between showgrounds in England. MMcF

Showman's steam traction engine model (c. 1980s),
H 35 x W 27 x L 57 cm

Treasures of the Museum

Punch and Judy mechanical bank

Punchinello, or Mr Punch, evolved from the plays performed by wandering troupes in 14th-century Italy. Punch acquired a wife, Judy (originally known as Joan), and by the mid-1800s the Punch and Judy Show was at the height of its popularity in Great Britain, Europe and America.

The mechanical bank is operated by pulling the lever, placing a coin in Judy's tray and then pressing the thumb piece. Judy turns and thrusts the coin into the bank as Punch approaches, swinging his club. This bank was owned by a child in Wonthaggi around 1900, and had been passed down through the family before being donated to the museum. It was originally finished in yellow, red, white and flesh-coloured paint with 'Punch and Judy Bank' inscribed across the stage. MMcF

Metters 'Moffat' electric stove

Around the late 1930s, a wealthy Geelong housewife, already the owner of an electric refrigerator and mix-master, purchased this Australian-made Metters 'Moffat' electric stove. The modern wife of a successful businessman, she represented the typical consumer of electrical goods at this time.

Astonishingly – in an era, when most households were not yet wired for electricity and when electrical appliances were still a luxury – the new stove was apparently used only once or twice to bake scones, and was then abandoned in disappointment. According to family lore, not even the cook was allowed to use it. The stove sat dormant in the kitchen for over 40 years, alongside the faithful old gas stove it was meant to replace.

When the stove came into the museum's collection, it was in almost new condition – a rare state for domestic appliances, which are generally marked by years of hard use. FK

Mechanical bank (c. 1890, base replaced c. 1980), cast iron, Shepard Hardware Co., H 18 x W 15.5 x D 10 cm

'Moffat' electric stove (c. 1930s), Metters KFB Pty Ltd, H 94 x W 94.5 x D 61 cm

Australian Society and Technology

Wax fruit and vegetables

These wax fruit and vegetable models, which date from the 1870s to the 1960s, look as if they have just been picked and are ready to eat. The collection fills 10 cabinets with over 50 types of fruits and vegetables, including 624 cultivars of apples, 94 pears and 135 plums.

In the absence of colour photography, the wax models were used to promote Victoria's horticultural development and opportunities. They were also used to educate the public about what was suitable for Victoria and to show the impact of common diseases and pests. The expertise of the museum staff who created this collection has been recognised internationally, and the models have been displayed in exhibitions overseas. LDH

A selection of the museum's large collection of wax fruit and vegetables

Treasures of the Museum

Washing machines

The museum's diverse collection of over 20 washing machines dates from the late 19th through to the late 20th century, and reflects a wide range of technological, social and environmental influences.

The distinctive, rocket-like Wolter & Echberg was designed and made in Australia in the late 19th century. Made of galvanised steel, its simple but innovative design used minimal water, but housewives still required a strong arm to swing it back and forth on wash day.

The 1930s electric Syracuse 'Easy' featured vacuum-cup technology, which helped force soapy water through clothes. The very name of this US-made twin tub machine reinforced the alluring, but not entirely true, promise from advertisers that electrical appliances would be labour saving.

The 1950s Thor 'Automagic' exploited the space-saving but novel idea of washing clothes and dishes in the same machine. Although innovative, this US-made machine still followed the 'white enamel box' form that was almost standard for domestic appliances by the 1940s.

The potential to use less water was a key factor of the 1950s Bendix 'Automatic Home Washer', as suggested by its 'water rationer' dial. Designed in the United Kingdom, this front-loading machine was an early example of concern about water and energy use, and the push for more environmentally efficient appliances.

This collection provides insights into historical issues such as domestic work, gender roles, design, manufacturing, consumer culture and sustainability. FK

1 'Easy' twin tub (1930s), Syracuse Washing Machine Corporation, H 99 x W 100 x D 72 cm

2 Compressed-air (late 19th century), Wolter & Echberg, H 66 x W 132 x D 65 cm

3 'Automagic' (1950s), Thor, H 95 x W 62 x D 62 cm

4 'Automatic Home Washer' (1950s), Bendix, 94 x W 68 x D 64 cm

5 Detail of the 'Easy' vacuum-cup technology

Australian Society and Technology

Archaeological material from 'Little Lon'

During the summer of 1987–88, historical archaeologists conducted an archaeological dig within part of the block bordered by Spring, Lonsdale, Exhibition and Little Lonsdale streets in Melbourne's central business district. The excavated area had an unsavoury reputation as a 'red light district' and as 'the heart of Melbourne's slumdom'.

The archaeologists uncovered the remains of lanes and pathways and the foundations of houses and workshops. They found thousands of objects used and discarded during the last third of the 19th century. Digs on other parts of the block during 2002 and 2003 recovered many other items.

The small houses accommodated families and single people, immigrants from Britain, China, Pakistan and Lebanon, children and the elderly. Within the diverse neighbourhood, two-roomed homes crowded together along narrow lanes, and factories, pubs, brothels and boarding houses attracted people from outside the area.

The collection provides fascinating insights into the people who lived and worked in Melbourne 140 years ago: the first generation of Europeans to settle the city. The archaeologists found magnums that once held the best French champagne. There were marbles, toy tea sets and a toy soldier; Chinese ceramics, willow-pattern plates, a Crimean War souvenir, tokens and coins. Residents purchased homoeopathic pain killers, patent medicines and laxatives. They ate mainly cheap cuts of mutton, and the area was infested with rats.

Archaeologists and historians continue to analyse the distribution and stratigraphy of objects, and discover more about the people who lived in the district. Did they live differently from those in other closely settled inner areas of 19th-century Australian cities? EW

Chinese coins from the Ch'ing (Manchu) dynasty (1662–1850), found wherever Chinese communities settled throughout the Pacific region

Clockwise from left: Mug, blue-and-white transfer printed, 'Italian' pattern (pre-1847), Copeland & Garrett, Staffordshire; saucer, mauve-and-white transfer printed earthenware, 'The Rhine' pattern (pre-1817), Dillwyn & Company, Swansea, Wales; lid for pot once containing 'bear's grease hair oil', polychromatic transfer ware; clay pipe, on one side a squatter takes his ease, on the other are two Aboriginal people drinking. The design is from an etching first published in 1838.

Stephanie Alexander

The recipe and remedy book of a resourceful woman

This household recipe and remedy book dates from the earliest years of settlement in rural Victoria. The author, Eliza Duckmanton, was born in 1843 and emigrated from England in 1859. She lived at Dunkeld near the Grampians until her death in 1924.

Eliza's book is fascinating, albeit a challenge to consult. There is no index or table of contents. Nor are the entries separated in any way. Biscuits abut pickles, which are followed by instructions on how to remove mildew from linen. Ginger beer recipes (of which there are several) are followed by instructions on how to dye white kid gloves purple and how to clean ribbons, followed by a recipe for lavender water.

Recipes for cakes and biscuits predominate, reflecting a world where all things British set the standard and where the quality of a woman's baking was a source of pride. The method in the recipes is often very scanty and would not satisfy many of today's less experienced cooks. A well-run colonial household would have had a store cupboard. The recipes for jams, jellies, relishes and sauces are among the most reliable in the collection, and modern versions of quince jelly and red currant jelly are no improvement on Eliza Duckmanton's recipes. Interestingly, there are almost no savoury recipes, other than for relishes or pickles. And no mention of using any indigenous ingredients as was a feature of some of the first cookery books published in Australia.

Living in an isolated rural household meant that one had to be resourceful. As the mother of 13 children, Eliza must have been highly organised and she apparently was often consulted for remedies for common ailments. The book contains suggestions for relieving symptoms

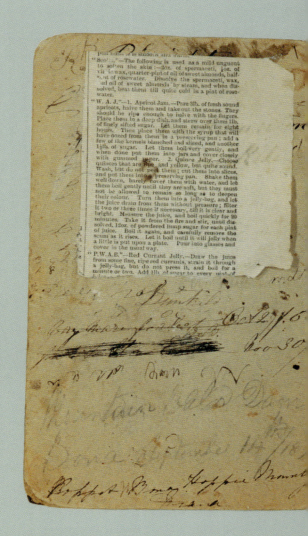

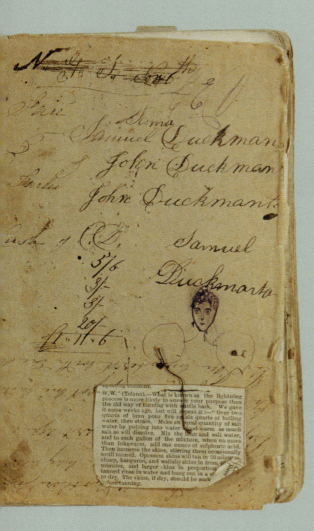

of conditions ranging from sore throats to cholera and cancer. One assumes that the book would have been handed on to some of Eliza's children. Indeed the different handwriting in the entries suggests that other family members contributed.

One looks in vain for much insight into or comment about daily life. Here and there is an initial, suggesting that a recipe came from someone else. I own a similar book, written by my grandmother between 1910 and 1920, and I found the likenesses quite striking, despite the distance of two generations. There are also differences. My grandmother's book is a record of friendships as much as it is a collection of recipes and household advice. This makes the one or two personal asides in Eliza's book even more delightful. Following her recipe 'To preserve eggs' is the note: 'I did not buy one egg this year. I had some preserved in this mixture. Just as they were finished our hens began to lay'.

Although the detail of daily life is absent, this book still has much to offer the student of social history. Those interested in cookery can study the repertoire of a colonial household and realise how many of the items are still well-loved today.

Stephanie Alexander is a food writer and a partner in Richmond Hill Cafe & Larder. The author of 10 books, she is one of Australia's most acclaimed food writers. Her fifth book, 'The Cook's Companion', is a kitchen bible in thousands of Australian homes.

Recipe and remedy book (late 19th century), H 18.5 x W 12.5 cm

Treasures of the Museum

Matchbook album

This album, put together by a Melbourne man during the 1930s, contains matchbooks issued predominantly by Melbourne businesses, such as department stores, hotels, restaurants, taxi companies and charities. Myer, Mario's Restaurant, the Menzies Hotel and Barnardo's, are represented, as are long-forgotten businesses such as Bell's Socks, the Tea Pot Inn, Blue Line Taxis and Garrick Cigarettes.

Matchbooks were a common form of advertising during most of the 20th century, until the perils of smoking hastened their decline. Usually given out free to customers and suppliers, matchbooks were designed to keep promoting a company while they lay around in people's homes or travelled around in their pockets. Matchbooks became a popular souvenir and collector's item, with many ending up in homes in glass jars, brandy balloons or albums such as this.

While each matchbook on its own might seem like nothing more than a novelty item, as a collection the album tells us much about the era when it was assembled. It presents us with a snapshot of commercial Melbourne between the First and Second World Wars, the graphics illustrating attitudes and ideals of the period. MR

Matchbook album (1930s), H 23 x W 18 cm

Australian Society and Technology

Electric telegraph network

In March 1854, the first public telegraph message in the Southern Hemisphere was transmitted in Melbourne. This was also the year the first railway line was opened in Melbourne, running from Flinders Street to Port Melbourne.

The electric telegraph network was the first system in which messages were sent over any distance by electrical means. It has been described as the first Internet. Manufactured in the United Kingdom, this single-needle instrument was one of the first telegraph devices developed. Needle telegraphs were used well into the 20th century, principally on railways. The needle telegraph predated the more prevalent morse system. The first public morse message was sent in 1847 in the United States; messages were recorded on paper tape. This model of a morse system includes a receiver employing paper tape. Paper tape was still being used by the first digital computers, such as CSIRAC, in the mid-20th century.

By 1902, the electric telegraph circled the world using submarine cable. The museum has cable samples from the first Atlantic cable laid in 1865. The cable shown was used between Victoria and Tasmania in the late 1800s.

A later feature of telegraph networks was mobile communication using wireless technology. The first mobile communication from Australia with a ship at sea was in May 1901, welcoming the Duke and Duchess of York to the celebration of Federation. The coherer was part of the land-based wireless telegraphy equipment. DD

Clockwise from top left: needle telegraph (c. 1840), Cook & Wheatstone, H 46 x W 25 x D 20 cm; morse system model (c. 1880), W. Myer, H 32 x W 54 x D 34 cm; cable (late 19th century), L 18 x diam. 3 cm; coherer (1901), W.H. Jenvey, H 5.5 x W 21.5 x L 8 cm

Detail of the morse system model

Bell double-pole magneto telephone

Alexander Graham Bell produced the first commercially viable telephone in 1876. In July of that year, at the Centennial Exhibition in Philadelphia, in the United States, he gave the first public demonstration of the telephone, using four different types of instrument.

It is not known when the first telephone message was transmitted in Australia, but there was much activity in developing telephony by the end of 1877. The telephone pictured here was constructed for Bell as part of a series of experiments carried out to refine his device. It was acquired by Bell's uncle, Edward Stace Symonds (Under Treasurer of Victoria from 1857 to 1887), during a visit to the Bell family in Canada in August 1876. Symonds brought the telephone and other items to Australia; the museum still possesses the wooden containers. The telephone was donated to the museum by Charles Osland Vandapear Moody in 1974. Charles' grandfather was a nephew of Symonds and a cousin of Bell. The donation included a description of an early telephone believed to be in Symonds' handwriting, and a tuned reed (or harmonic telegraph receiver) used by Bell in his experiments. DD

Left to right: Alexander Graham Bell and Thomas Watson, double-pole magneto telephone (c. 1876), H 17 x W 26.5 x D 16 cm; harmonic telegraph receiver (1870s), H 7.8 x W 14.5 x D 8 cm

Australian Society and Technology

Triunial projector

The triunial, or triple, projector is part of the David Francis Collection. The internationally significant collection traces moving picture technology from the mid-17th century to the silent movie era in the late 1920s.

Lantern slide shows were the historical equivalent of modern multimedia presentations. Magical effects of great sophistication were created. With double or triple projectors, clothed human beings could be morphed into skeletons that crumbled to dust. A landscape could be ravaged by winds, ripped apart by floods or seen to change gradually with the passing of the seasons. DD

Sutton panoramic camera

This beautiful and precisely constructed camera enabled a photographer to capture more of the magnificence of an evocative landscape than was possible with a flat plate camera. The panoramic effect was achieved with curved glass plates and a hollow glass lens filled with distilled water, resulting in a photograph spanning 140 degrees. The blank plate was dipped in emulsion in the sensitising tank and the photograph was taken while the plate was still wet.

The museum possesses 12 curved glass negatives taken by Richard Daintree, a pioneer of Australian fieldwork photography. The camera was designed in England by Thomas Sutton; about 30 were made. DD

Triunial projector (late 19th century), J. Ottway & Son, H 110 x W 50 x L 90 cm

Thomas Sutton, panoramic camera (c. 1861), with glass negative and sensitising tank, H 28 x W 35 x D 31 cm

Robyn Williams

The last original brain machine

On 25 November 1999, I was on my way to dinner at The Lodge. With my customary, irritating promptness, I arrived first and found Prime Minister John Howard standing alone in the garden.

'Good evening,' I offered randomly. 'Do you realise that on this very day 50 years ago the first computer in Australia, CSIRAC, came into operation?' The PM was impressed. 'It was the fourth stored-memory computer in the world and the first to generate music!', I continued.

I was running out of my own stored memory. Luckily the then CSIRO boss, Sir Malcolm Mackintosh, arrived and provided a wealth of further CSIRAC information.

CSIRAC was the brainchild of Trevor Pearcey, a physicist who came from Britain in 1945, part of the team of radar 'boffins' who were to transform southern radio astronomy. The aim was to build a machine for experimental computing. Pearcey designed it, Maston Beard, an Australian engineer, built it. CSIRAC, when finished, weighed two tonnes, covered 40 square metres and was made up of nine steel cabinets containing 2000 valves. It required enough electric power to run a village. CSIRAC was at the cutting edge of modern computing, having been preceded only by SSEM (1948) and EDSAC (1949) in Britain and BINAC (1949) in the United States. Yet this behemoth could manage only 0.001 megahertz (compared with 500 in your PC) and 2000 bytes (compared with 64 megabytes plus 10 000 million in stored memory).

CSIRO Division of Building research staff at work on CSIRAC, 1958
Source: CSIRO, Division of Building, Construction and Engineering

Trevor Pearcey working on CSIRAC, 1951
Source: CSIRO, Division of Building, Construction and Engineering

Nonetheless, CSIRAC was able to perform impressively, calculating weather forecasts, bank loans, star positions, the flow of rivers in the Snowy Mountains Scheme, building designs, and producing the world's first computer music. Geoff Hill, CSIRAC's programmer, came from a musical family and, beginning in 1951, had the computer perform 'Colonel Bogey' and 'Auld Lang Syne'. Was this the start of the multimedia revolution?

After a spell at the University of Sydney in the Radiophysics Division, CSIRAC was loaded onto a vast truck and carried to Melbourne, where it gave a range of services for nine more years, offering the first computer courses in a university. Then came the transistor and, after 15 years of excellent service, CSIRAC was finally turned off in 1964. This grand engine, a descendant of Charles Babbage's 19th-century dream, had used punched cards and paper tape and was puny compared to the gadget in your pocket, but it had given Australia a lead in modern computing.

Trevor Pearcey believed that this lead was relinquished when CSIRAC's example was not followed up. Others insist it gave Australia an invaluable computer culture, which remains strong today. Whatever the heritage, the engine still stands, the only one of its kind fully preserved. Be impressed, whether you are a prime minister, a computer buff, or like me simply enthralled by still-living history. But don't ask to switch it on. After 40 years of rest, CSIRAC would now probably blow up.

Robyn Williams is a broadcast journalist and science writer. He presents 'The Science Show' each week on ABC Radio National, has written 10 books, including a novel, and is a fellow of the Australian Academy of Science.

The grid of lights at the top of the image were one means by which staff monitored CSIRAC

The valves (vacuum tubes) were part of the 'brain' of CSIRAC – the central processing unit

Immigration and material culture

Immigration is about all non-Indigenous Australians, whether we arrived yesterday or our ancestors arrived 200 years ago. We all have our origins in another country and another culture.

Since 1990, the museum has collected objects that help represent and interpret the social, political and economic issues at the heart of any immigrant society. Artefacts are valuable in representing ordinary as well as extraordinary lives, allowing us to explore and rediscover the experiences of women, workers, immigrants and children in both historical and contemporary contexts.

We can follow a person's journey and the artefacts, memories and cultural identity he or she brings; we can represent the experiences of settlement at both a personal and broader social level; we can look at immigration policies and processes and how they have developed over time.

When we consider an immigration collection, we might immediately think of suitcases and trunks. A potent symbol of the immigrant experience is what people could bring and what they had to leave behind. There are many luggage items in the collection, ranging from trunks that journeyed by sea from England in 19th-century clippers and steamers, to suitcases crammed into the holds of 1950s European ocean liners, to a vinyl bag owned by a Vietnamese refugee who arrived by aeroplane in the 1970s. Luggage can hold belongings of personal, professional and symbolic significance. The museum has collected a pocket-sized photo album, a family Bible, a child's doll, a set of work tools, a loom and numerous other precious and familiar items for starting a new life.

Immigration has always been about paper. Identity papers have meant acceptance or rejection for immigrants in any era. Policy documents trace the shifts in government philosophy about who can come to Australia and how – and who cannot and why. Application forms reflect the evolving bureaucratic processes of immigration. Shipboard menus, activity programs and newsletters tell us what people ate during their journey and how they amused themselves. Diaries and scrapbooks capture the memories of departure, separation, journey, arrival and first impressions of the new homeland.

The development of the immigration collection demonstrates that the simplest object can tell the most moving story. The museum holds a small set of house keys – mundane, ordinary, common. Yet they are also the only items grabbed by a couple as they fled Hungary in 1956. Suddenly they become unique, precious, and full of meaning for the couple who have given them to the museum and to thousands of people with stories just like it, in different times and different places. MMcF

A selection of the museum's traditional Greek shadow puppets. Dimitris Katsoulis, a master of the genre, migrated to Melbourne in 1974, hoping to foster the tradition in Australia. Greek shadow puppetry evolved from the Turkish model, which dates back to at least the 16th century. The central figure is the roguish Karaghiozis (main image), and he and a variety of characters are involved in humorous moral tales that make satirical observations about social and political life.
Courtesy of Dimitri Katsoulis

Australian Society and Technology

31

Cuc Lam's suitcase

In 1978, Cuc Lam fled Vietnam with her husband, Minh, in a rickety fruit and vegetable boat. Refugees carry little, if anything, with them, and what they do is often lost or thrown away. Cuc's small, red vinyl suitcase is inscribed with her name and travel details, indicating her journey to Melbourne from Malaysia by plane. She sacrificed her wedding ring to buy the case so that she would not arrive in Australia empty-handed. Cuc and Minh dressed in well-worn shirts and shorts to disguise themselves as fishers during their escape from Vietnam. These and other tiny keepsakes are also in the museum's collection.

An historical artefact is only as powerful as the story that comes with it. Cuc Lam's suitcase symbolises the individual and collective memories of thousands of refugees now living in Australia. MMcF

Vinyl suitcase with original baggage tag and cloth identification label (1970s), H 46 x L 46 x D 15 cm

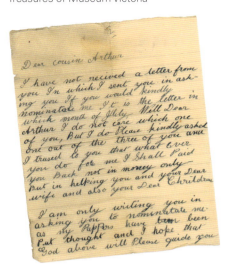

Letter from Thomasina Tye to Arthur Tye

This poignant plea from Thomasina Tye to her cousin Arthur offers a personal insight into the plight of people who have struggled to migrate to Australia. The letter, an uncommon example from the 1920s, reveals a desperate call for assistance, and also documents immigration application and selection processes. Only through a guarantee of good character and support will she be given approval to migrate from England to Australia.

Thomasina writes '. . . I hope that God above alone will Please guide you or one of . . . nominatate me as I have been told again to make a move, from hear . . . I am detirmed to come my mind is made up in coming out to Aus' (original spelling).

Letters provide us with a personal voice and a personal touch – paper, handwriting, tone and expression. But did Thomasina ever make it? MMcF

Two-page letter sent from Birmingham, England, to Australia (22 November 1928)

Australian Society and Technology

Timber photograph album covers

These photograph album covers are one set of two made by Orion Wenhrynowycz with tools he brought from the Ukraine. In 1948, Mr Wenhrynowycz and his wife immigrated to Australia on the *Wooster Victory* as displaced persons, under the Labor government's post–Second World War immigration scheme. Upon arrival at Station Pier, Melbourne, the couple were immediately put on a train that took them to the Bonegilla Migrant Reception Centre in north-eastern Victoria. At Bonegilla, waiting to be placed on his two-year work contract and undergoing an 'Australianisation' program, Orion Wenhrynowycz put his wood-crafting skills to use. MT

Walnut and cherrywood mandolin

From their earliest migration to Melbourne, Italian immigrants have had a strong connection to the performing arts. Giovanni Cera came to Australia in 1922 from Asiago, Italy. A self-taught musician, he and several compatriots formed the Tango Orchestra, which performed regularly on the ABC radio station 3LO during the 1930s and 1940s. He also played in the Tivoli Orchestra, accompanying silent movies. Cera's passion for stringed instruments, and in particular for the mandolin, violin and guitar, led him to design and craft his own instruments in the quest for creating the perfect sound. This mandolin, carved from walnut and cherrywood, was made in a purpose-built workshop at his home in Carlton, where he lived and worked for over 50 years. MT

Photograph album covers (1948), H 28 x W 19 cm

Mandolin (1930), H 6.4 x W 24 x L 66.4 cm

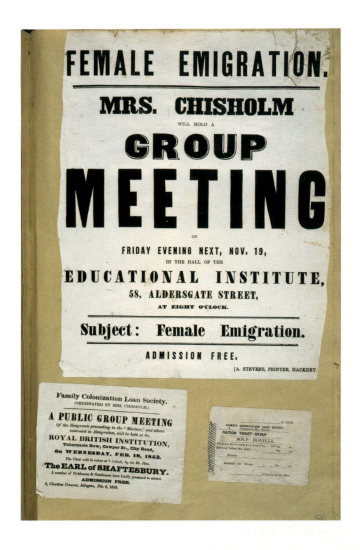

Treasures of the Museum

Caroline Chisholm scrapbook

Caroline Chisholm, 19th-century social reformer and philanthropist, left few personal effects to shed light on her remarkable life. This scrapbook, handed down through the Chisholm family, was purchased by a Chisholm historian at an auction in Tasmania, and in 2000 was presented to the museum.

The scrapbook consists of material relating to Chisholm's work assisting immigrants in, or trying to get to, Australia: newspaper clippings, public notices, posters, correspondence, her Family Colonization Loan Society constitution and meeting minutes, and documents containing her signature. The earliest document dates back to 1843; most of the items are from her time in Britain and Australia from 1852 to 1866.

It is not known who collated the scrapbook. Perhaps it was Chisholm herself, but it might also have been her husband, Archibald, or one of her nine children. The personal nature of much of the material, such as soiree invitations and railway tickets, suggests the compiler was someone intimate with her personal archive. The items are not in chronological order, but were probably added shortly after the events they record.

The scrapbook captures Chisholm's working life. Posters advertise the immigration lectures she gave across Great Britain; railway tickets stamped for free travel indicate the distances she covered and the official support for her project; invitation cards reveal a woman circulating in high society, where her fundraising efforts would have been directed; lists of names record the people she assisted financially to migrate to Australia.

The ephemera of a life, so easily dispersed and discarded, have been preserved for perpetuity in a humble ledger. MMcF

Scrapbook (c. 1860–70), H 50.5 x W 31.5 cm

PICTORIAL PAGES.

people generally. When at one time hesitating whether her unaided efforts could be of any service in the cause of humanity, an incident occurred which nerved her resolution. A young and beautiful Highland girl, soon after her arrival in the colony, met the unfortunate fate of too many. A providential accident brought Mrs. Chisholm across her path when she was about to commit suicide. "I did not leave the place," she said, "until I heard her, with subdued feelings, vow never again to attempt self-destruction. I provided her lodgings; my spirit returned—I felt God's blessing was on my work. *From the time I was on the beach with Flora fear left me.*"

As soon as the "Home" was established, Mrs. Chisholm determined, as she had done under similar circumstances in Madras, to reside on the premises. The room appropriated to her private use by the government was not more than seven feet square. The following is her account of taking possession. "Having been busy all day, I retired to rest; my courage was put to the proof at starting. Scarce was the light out, when I fancied, from a noise I heard, that dogs must be in the room, and in some terror I got a light. What I experienced in seeing rats in all directions I cannot describe! My first act was to throw on a cloak and get at the door, with the intent of leaving the building. My second thoughts were, that if I did so, my desertion would cause much amusement, and ruin my plan. I therefore lighted a second candle, and seating myself on my bed, kept there until the rats descending from the roof alighted on my shoulders. I felt that I was getting into a fever, and, in fact, that I should be very ill before morning; but to be *out-generalled by rats* was too bad! I got up with some resolution. I had two loaves and some butter, (for my office, bed-room, and pantry were one,) I cut the bread into slices, placed the whole in the middle of the room, and, with a light by my side, I kept my seat on the bed, reading Abercrombie, and watching the rats till four in the morning. I at one time counted thirteen, and never less than seven, did I observe at the dish during the entire night. The following night I gave them a similar treat, with the addition of arsenic, and in this manner I passed my first four nights at the "Home."

The "Home" having been established and rendered prosperous, Mrs. Chisholm continued to prosecute her benevolent mission in rendering timely aid to emigrants. She undertook journeys of three hundred miles into the interior with families. "The largest number," she says, "that ever left Sydney under my charge was one hundred and forty-seven persons, but by accessions on the road they increased considerably!"

In 1846, Mrs. Chisholm was rejoined by her husband, and returned to England, where she has ever since remained, acting in the same spirit and for the same important object—the prosperity and happiness of Emigrants.

MRS. CHISHOLM.

Australian Society and Technology

Stained-glass window

Around 1872, James Fergusson moved into his new home, Glenferrie, in Malvern, then on the eastern edge of Melbourne. It was a fine two-storey brick mansion, with 14 rooms and extensive grounds. Fergusson was general manager of Fergusson & Mitchell, one of the leading printing firms and manufacturing stationers in the Colony of Victoria, and he had recently been elected a Member of the Legislative Assembly.

Fergusson commissioned a large, stained-glass stairwell window for his new home, almost certainly from the Melbourne firm Ferguson & Urie; several similar examples of the company's work from the 1860s to 1880s survive in Melbourne churches and mansions.

The images in the window reflect the commercial wealth and confidence of a generation of immigrants that had come to the young colony and made its fortune through agriculture, mining, manufacturing and trade. Painted glass panels depict shipping, railways, farming, mining, commerce and, personally significant to Fergusson, printing. The window is also a symbol of the colony's pride and its continuing attachment to Britain.

At the top of the window, a kangaroo and an emu stand on either side of the Australian colonial coat-of-arms. Pride of place in the middle of the window is given to the Fergusson Blazon of Arms, with three boars' heads and a buckle. The thistle, rose and shamrock (symbols respectively of Scotland, England and Ireland) are repeated throughout the background.

After James Fergusson's death in 1888, Glenferrie passed through several owners, until it was eventually demolished in 1954. A local resident apparently purchased the window and built it into their modern home in the 1970s. When new owners undertook extensive renovations in 2001, they donated the window to the museum. RG

Stained-glass window (c. 1872), Ferguson & Urie, H 334 x W 191 cm
Glenferrie (subsequently called Zeerust), possibly shortly before its demolition in 1954. The Fergusson arms sit above the second-storey windows.
Source: Royal Historical Society of Victoria

Treasures of the Museum

Biggest Family Album in Australia

The Biggest Family Album in Australia is a unique collection of photographs of everyday people engaged in everyday activities. Dating from as early as 1850 and spanning more than 100 years, the collection portrays Victorians at home, at work and at play. These are not the famous or powerful but rather ordinary families, shopkeepers, farmers, soldier settlers, Murray River boatmen, miners in the goldfields and people in towns and country areas.

Initiated in the early 1980s, the project was a significant departure from the traditional practice of collecting photographs based on artistic merit or the photographer's reputation. Instead, museum staff travelled extensively through regional areas, inviting families to look through their albums and select images for inclusion in the project. More than 9500 submissions were carefully copied, the information supplied with each image recorded on a database and originals returned to their owners. The people of Victoria were given both ownership and authorship of their heritage.

A first in many ways, this project also marked a significant change in information management at the museum, piloting the introduction of computer-based access to images and related data.

In keeping with its community focus, the project culminated in a number of books and a series of regional exhibitions showcasing local images. The collection has a continuing role in enriching contemporary understanding of who we are, and providing an invaluable visual resource for historians, students, researchers, publishers and genealogists alike. AR

Shopping at Barrell's Grocery store, Sturt Street, Ballarat, c. 1930

A kerosene-powered motor car built by William Toy motor car manufacturer, Stud Road, Dandenong, 1908

Australian Society and Technology

Apinis loom

Looms are symbols of artistic skill, cultural maintenance and universal female traditions. Latvian weavers Anna Apinis and Elga Kivicka had looms made for them by male displaced persons in their camp in postwar Germany, using wood scavenged from bombed-out ruins. Anna sketched and documented ancient Latvian designs from the regional costumes rescued by other Latvian refugee women. She then wove them on her loom with threads gathered from unravelled scraps of old fabric.

Anna was able to bring her precious loom when she migrated to Australia in 1950. Her weaving helped to ease the pain of displacement and separation she and her husband Ervins felt in their new land. As suitable weaving materials were difficult to find in postwar Australia, Ervins designed an unplying machine while the couple were living in Parkes Holding Centre in Canberra in 1950. Made from cans, scrap metal and wood, he used the machine to unply balls of wool to make weaving threads.

Anna became one of the few suppliers of fabric for Latvian national costumes in Australia in the 1950s and 1960s, and she showed her weaving nationally, at exhibitions and Latvian cultural festivals. She fulfilled her dream to keep her cultural traditions alive through her daughter, Anita, who continues to weave on Anna's loom.

This is Elga's loom, similar to Anna's and purchased by Anna in the 1970s for her own use. MMcF

Anna Apinis teaches weaving at Memmingen Displaced Persons Camp, 1947
Courtesy of the Apinis Family
Detail of countermarch floor loom (c. 1947), H 188 x W 143 x D 170 cm
Technical drawing of the loom by Ervinis Apinis forms the watermark
Courtesy of the Apinis Family

Trade literature collection

Trade literature can be broadly defined as the publications prepared by a company to promote, distribute, explain and maintain its product lines. It typically includes promotional brochures, product catalogues, repair and maintenance manuals, price lists, accessory and parts lists, specification sheets and technical bulletins.

At the time of writing, the museum's trade literature collection contained more than 30 000 items and spanned more than 150 years of manufacturing history both within Australia and internationally.

The value of the trade literature collection extends far beyond a simple catalogue of equipment available at a given time. It enables us to gain insights into the economy, working conditions and social tastes of an era. Manufacturing techniques are described or illustrated. We can identify product successes and failures, track the growth of Australian export markets and understand the impact of imported technologies on Australian companies. The breadth of subjects (ranging from watches to earth-moving equipment, domestic appliances to precision chemical apparatus and horseworks to military aircraft) makes it possible to trace the formation, development and ultimately globalisation of Australian industry.

The collection complements the objects held by the museum, expanding our knowledge of those items. Long after the machines, equipment, transport and appliances have ended their useful working lives or faded into obscurity, the detailed descriptions, specifications, diagrams and images found in trade literature can continue to inform. AR

Australian Society and Technology

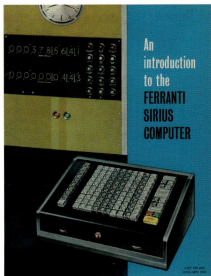

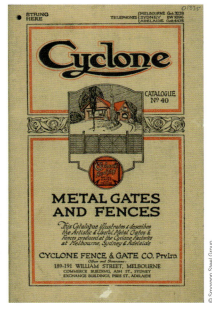

A sample of catalogues from the museum's collection of trade literature (1905–61)

Treasures of the Museum

Working models case

Interactive exhibits have always been part of the museum's technological collections. For those who remember a visit to the old Swanston Street site, one of the highlights was the large working models case filled with an intriguing clutter of mechanical delights. Although just another piece of exhibition hardware when first installed in the 1920s, over the decades it became so steeped in the memories of generations of visitors that it acquired the status of a collection object in its own right.

Part of the marvel of the case was the drive mechanism originally designed by Professor Wilfred Kernot of the University of Melbourne, who helped install and activate the first four models. Over the years the layout and contents of the case evolved, but the principle remained the same. Each model was powered by a leather belt from a common overhead shaft and could be started by pushing a numbered button to engage the appropriate dog clutch.

The models themselves have interesting origins. The oldest, a portable steam engine and a horizontal stationary engine, were made by Ransomes & Sims of Ipswich, England, in 1859, as fully steamable models depicting the firm's full-size products. Another 14 models depicting governors, ratchets and other mechanisms were part of a group of 120 models that the museum ordered in 1915 from G. Cussons of Manchester.

During the 1930s, the case was supplemented with further models, including miniature marine engines built by James Struthers of Renfrew, Scotland, and intricate models of a Maudslay table engine and rotative beam engine built as a hobby by A.E. Smith, the chief mechanical engineer of the Victorian Railways. The rotative beam engine is reported to depict an engine that was used to supply hydraulic power at the Williamstown Patent Slip in the 1860s. MC

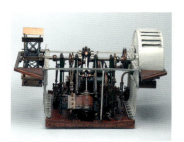  

Sectional model of compound diagonal paddle-steamer engine (1934), James Struthers, H 45 x W 72 x D 62 cm

Rotative beam engine model (c. 1930), A.E. Smith, H 28 x W 34.5 x D 16 cm

Working models case on display at National Museum of Victoria, c.1965

Museum Victoria Collection

Australian Society and Technology

Spotswood Pumping Station

Despite its grand facades and tree-lined boulevards, 19th-century Melbourne was not always a healthy or pleasant place to live. Foul-smelling effluent from noxious industries flowed freely into rivers and waterways, and untreated sewage could be found overflowing backyard cesspits and running down street gutters. By the late 1880s, the rising death rate from outbreaks of waterborne diseases such as typhoid and diphtheria finally prompted the government into action.

In 1891, the Melbourne & Metropolitan Board of Works was formed, and construction of the city's first centralised sewerage system began. From its official opening in February 1898, the Spotswood Pumping Station served for 67 years as the heart of Melbourne's sewerage system, pumping wastewater collected in underground sewers from homes, factories, stables and businesses to a treatment farm at Werribee.

During its working years, the pumping station had a distinctly maritime feel. Many of the engineers and labourers were recruited from maritime industries and took a great interest in the daily parade of ships passing along the river to and from Melbourne's docks. Today, the former Spotswood Pumping Station at Scienceworks is one of Australia's foremost industrial heritage sites, incorporating an internationally significant collection of late 19th- and early 20th-century pumping equipment, including two original steam boilers and five triple-expansion pumping engines together with centrifugal pumps, electric motors and control equipment. Enriching this technology is an associated collection of over 1000 artefacts, from tools to furniture, and a similar number of photographs, documents and oral histories recording almost every aspect of the site's history and every hour of its working life. MC

Spotswood Pumping Station pictured from the Yarra riverfront, 1938
Museum Victoria Collection

View down No 6 well, showing one of the first electric centrifugal pumps, installed in 1921
Photographer: David Loram, DDL Photographics

Clunes quartz mining model

This model depicts the mine and treatment works of the Port Phillip & Colonial Gold Mining Company at Clunes, once the most famous goldmine in Australia and a pioneer in large-scale mining of low-grade quartz ore. It was the last and most ambitious of 10 scale models that the Swedish-born miner and artisan Carl Nordström made for the museum in the late 1850s, depicting aspects of early Victorian goldmining. The model was commissioned by Fredrick McCoy in April 1858 and took over six months to complete at a cost of £215, over twice Nordström's initial estimate.

Nordström built the model 'on location' at the mine site and was assisted by the company's manager, Rivett Bland, and the company's engineer in perfecting details of the machinery and underground workings. He used materials at hand on the goldfields, such as plaster of Paris, hessian, wire, candle wax, sheet lead and timber from packing crates. He made each figure and piece of machinery in exact proportion to its actual size at a scale of ⅜ inch to a foot (1 in 32), while cleverly reducing the overall size of the model by shortening the relative distance between various features on the site.

When first displayed in Melbourne in early 1859, the model so impressed a reporter from the *Argus* that he described it as unsurpassed in 'boldness of ... design, minuteness of detail, and beauty of execution'. In the decades since, the Clunes model has continued to fascinate and delight succeeding generations of museum visitors. While McCoy commissioned the model with a view to educating 'new chum' miners in the most up-to-date mining technology, he also created a unique historical artefact, capturing details of early Victorian mining technology unrecorded in other pictorial and written accounts. MC

Carl Nordström, scale model of Clunes quartz mine and treatment works (1858), H 185 x W 165 x D 305 cm

Australian Society and Technology

Amalgamated Society of Carpenters and Joiners eight-hour banner

In April 1914, the new banner of the Victorian District of the Amalgamated Society of Carpenters and Joiners (ASCJ) debuted in Melbourne's annual eight-hour day procession.

Made by W.G. Dunstan, the side of the banner shown depicts the ASCJ membership certificate. Originating in Britain, the certificate includes tableaux of carpentry and joinery, surrounded by allegorical figures of Truth, Justice, Industry, Art, Peace and Friendship, as well as depictions of a carpenter and joiner. It is crowned by the society's shield and Joseph of Nazareth, history's most distinguished carpenter. Its motto, *Credo Sed Caveo*, advises, 'Believe, but take heed'.

The procession, first held in May 1856, celebrated the proclamation by Melbourne's skilled building workers of an eight-hour working day three weeks earlier, on 21 April. Claiming that a reduced working day would improve their health and 'social and moral condition', the unionists marched behind a banner declaring 'Eight hours' work, eight hours' rest, eight hours' recreation', from 'Carlton Paddock' in Melbourne to a fete at Cremorne Gardens in Melbourne's south. Legislated as a public holiday in 1879, the procession became Melbourne's biggest, peaking just before the First World War, and superseded by Moomba in the 1950s. MMcC

W.G. Dunstan, ASCJ Victorian District banner (1914), H 420 x W 360 cm
Courtesy of the Construction, Forestry, Mining and Energy Union, Victorian Branch

The Numismatics Collection

The museum's collection of coins, paper money and medals shows how the individual interests of curators and private collectors can, over time, build an internationally significant collection.

The Numismatics Collection includes medals and coins from the private collection of Eugene von Guerard, notable Victorian artist and first curator of the Numismatics Collection in 1871. His collection reflected the prevailing interest in coins from antiquity as well as more recent European coins.

As Australia moved towards nationhood in the late 19th century, Australian coins and trade tokens became the focus of increasing interest. This was reflected in a 1903 bequest from George McArthur of almost 2000 Australian pieces, and acquisitions by a new curator of the Numismatics Collection, Alfred Chitty, appointed in 1917. Concurrently, the Melbourne Mint built an extensive collection of reference pieces of Australian and foreign coins and medals through exchange with other mints, initially for its displays at the international exhibitions held in Melbourne in 1880 and 1888. In the 1970s, the museum combined the National Gallery and Melbourne Mint collections into a single state collection.

The Numismatics Collection also has a rich diversity of commemorative medals, awards, military medals and art medals. They include an early Victoria Cross awarded during the British campaign in Abyssinia in 1868 (part of the important Wannemacher donation in 1930), Art Deco medals by French and Belgian artists, and commemorative and prize medals from Melbourne's international exhibitions.

Comprising almost 100 000 items, the collection is now the most significant numismatics collection in Australia, with unique reference material from Australia and overseas. RG

1–3

4–8

9–13

14–18

19–23

Australian Society and Technology

1 Victoria Cross (1868), Queen Victoria, Great Britain, H 9 x W 4 cm. This Victoria Cross was awarded to Drummer Michael Magner for his brave attack during the Abyssinia Campaign.

2 Polar medal (1912–14), Great Britain, H 11.2 x W 3.5 cm. This medal was awarded to John Henry Collison Close, who took part in Mawson's Antarctic expedition on the *Aurora*.

3 MacRobertson International Air Race (1934), Australia, H 9 x W 3.6 cm. The race, from London to Melbourne, was sponsored by businessman and philanthropist Sir MacPherson Robertson. This gilt medal may have been awarded to members of ground staff or distributed as a promotional effort.

4 Silver stater (400–350 BC), ancient Greek city-state of Corinth, diam. 2.1 cm. The stater was a basic unit of the ancient Greek coinage system. Its exact value varied between the Greek states.

5 Silver didrachm (258–202 BC), ancient Greek city-state of Ephesus, diam. 2.1 cm

6 Aureus, Tiberius, (14–37 AD), Roman Empire, diam. 1.8 cm. The aureus was the basic unit of ancient Roman gold coinage for over three centuries.

7 Gold quarter stater, (c. 125 BC), Celtic Britain, diam. 1.3 cm

8 Ecu (1336–77), Edward III, Great Britain, diam. 2.8 cm

9 Ducat (1343–54), Venice, Italy, diam. 2 cm. A ducat was an important trade coin used in the eastern Mediterranean region.

10 Unite (1603–25), James VI, Scotland, diam. 3.6 cm. The denomination called 'unite' was introduced to commemorate the unification of England and Scotland under a single crown.

11 Two pounds (1820), George III, Great Britain, diam. 2.8 cm. This design was later used on sovereigns made by Australian mints.

12 Two Rumi Altin, 1223 year 9 AH (1817), Mahmud II, Ottoman Empire, diam. 2.9 cm

13 Five shillings or 'holey dollar' (1813), Australia, diam. 3.9 cm. In 1813, the New South Wales colonial government overcame an acute shortage of currency by punching out the centres of Spanish silver dollars (then worth five shillings) and creating two new coins – the 'holey dollar' (valued at five shillings) and the 'dump' (valued at one shilling and three pence).

14 Penny, pattern (1920), George V, Australia, H 1.8 x W 1.8 cm. This was part of a series of experiments to find a replacement for the large bronze penny. The square shape was based on a current coin from Ceylon (present-day Sri Lanka).

15 Penny, proof (1930), George V, Australia, diam. 2.6 cm. During the Depression, no 1930 pennies were issued by the Commonwealth. However, some were struck by the Melbourne Mint to test dies in case orders were received from the Commonwealth. The proof 1930 penny is Australia's most valuable coin.

16 Penny token (1850), artist J.C. Thornthwaite, New South Wales, diam. 3.5 cm. This was the first attempt to manufacture a token in Australia.

17 Melbourne Exhibition 1854 prize, artist Joseph S. Wyon, Australia, diam. 6.4 cm. This was won by the museum for its display of 'minerals, natural history etc'.

18 Exposition Universelle, Paris (1867), artist P.J.H. Ponscarme, France, diam. 3.7 cm. Sir Redmond Barry led a Victorian delegation to the Paris Exposition Universelle in 1867. He was presented this gold medal by the exhibition commissioners.

19 Melbourne International Exhibition prize medal, pattern (1880), artist Harry Stokes, Australia, diam. 7.6 cm. This is the medal pattern entered by Harry Stokes for the 1880 Melbourne International Exhibition prize medal competition.

20 San Francisco Earthquake (1906), artist Louis Bottee, France, diam. 9 cm

21 Tower Bridge (1924), artist Percy Metcalfe, Great Britain, diam. 6.4 cm

22 Stations of the Cross – Crucifixion (1943), artist Andor Meszaros, Australia, diam. 6.4 cm. One of the 'Canterbury Series' of medals prepared for Canterbury Cathedral, England.

23 Waterford Cathedral cast seal (early 1860s), Ireland, diam. 6 cm. Part of an original group of casts manufactured for display at the museum.

Objects from the Department of Psychiatric Services

Objects collected from several Victorian psychiatric institutions tell a sad story of neglect and the lack of political will. Much of the museum's collection was assembled during the 1950s by Dr Charles Brothers while he was working within the system to bring about reforms.

Victoria's first 'lunatic asylum' was a bluestone barracks in extensive grounds at Yarra Bend. By the late 1860s, the colony's population of people with psychiatric disabilities, including confused and dementing elderly people, had increased enormously. Between 1867 and 1872, the government opened three institutions, at Kew, Beechworth and Ararat, as shelter for 'lunatics'. The buildings were huge, with large dormitories and kitchens, and extensive gardens and farmlands. Capable patients could learn and work at a trade, and a strict routine was followed, with the aim of 'imposing order on chaotic minds'.

Soon these institutions were themselves overcrowded, and attempts to separate patients by type of illness faltered. The asylum population comprised people with intellectual disabilities, confused elderly, and those with psychiatric illnesses. Treatments included restriction, isolation and sometimes sedation, and there was limited contact with families and friends. Some people were calmed by the regular routine and the break from outside responsibility and were able to be discharged, but many stayed in institutions until they died.

Dr Brothers' investigations uncovered the institutionalised poverty and lack of hope resulting from decades of government and community neglect. The texture of daily life in an impoverished and overcrowded institution is evoked by well-worn domestic objects, battered metal chamber pots and standardised clothing. EW

Straightjacket (pre-1940), L 91 × W 49 cm

ECT machine (1940), H 27 × W 44.5 × D 29 cm

Australian Society and Technology

Ancient Order of Foresters' banner

This early banner from an Australian friendly society was produced for the members of the 'Court Unity' of the Ancient Order of Foresters, who met in Ballarat. It shows the emblem of the Foresters, with their motto, *Unitas Benevolentia et Concordia* (United in Charity and Friendship).

In a world without social security, working men could see the value of joining friendly societies. At the regular lodge meeting, members would pay a small subscription, a form of insurance that would entitle them to benefits if they became ill or unemployed, and would provide support for their dependents if members died. They identified proudly with their society, wearing elaborate regalia at meetings and learning complicated initiation rites and the rituals associated with membership.

This banner was made by artist and photographer Thomas Flintoff (1809–91) in his Ballarat workshop. It is painted in oil on green taffeta backed with cotton, and has a wide white border edged with brocade. Banners such as this were hung in the meeting rooms of lodges, and were carried by lodge members in regalia during civic processions and celebrations.

Thomas Flintoff worked in Ballarat between 1856 and 1872, and then in Melbourne. The museum has two of his banners. He also produced 'infallotypes' (photographic images highlighted with oil paint) and oil portraits of many of the colony's leading citizens. EW

Thomas Flintoff, 'Ancient Order of Foresters/ No 3200/ Court Unity/ Ballarat' (c. 1860), H 376 x W 292 cm

Royal Exhibition Building

The Royal Exhibition Building is a product of the optimism, enthusiasm and energy of the people of Melbourne in the late 19th century. In 1879, when the foundation stone was laid, Melbourne was an extremely prosperous city, basking in the wealth from the richest gold rush in the world. The future seemed unlimited, and Victorians wanted to publicise their achievements in an international exhibition. The building was designed by Joseph Reed and erected in less than 18 months.

The first exhibition opened on 1 October 1880. The excited crowd included many who had immigrated during the 1850s gold rush. They had seen Melbourne change from a scatter of wooden houses to a marvellous modern city. The new Exhibition Building, the largest building in Australia, was a symbol of their confidence in the future.

The 1880–81 International Exhibition attracted entries from 33 countries and over a million visitors. The boom times continued, and in 1888 at the Centennial Exhibition, annexes full of displays covered the gardens north to Carlton Street, and people made 2 million visits.

In 1901, after Federation, a crowd of 12 000 watched while the first federal parliament was opened with great ceremony in the Great Hall. The recently restored interior replicates the decorative scheme designed for that event. Trade fairs, motor shows, balls, meetings, flower shows, examinations and rock concerts have all been held here. The building's significance as the only surviving 'Palace of Industry' from the World Fair movement has been recognised by its nomination for UNESCO's World Heritage List. The Royal Exhibition Building is now part of Museum Victoria. EW

Melbourne's new Exhibition Building, *Illustrated London News*, 14 February 1880

Southern façade of the Exhibition Building, c. 1901
Museum Victoria Collection

Interior of dome and Great Hall of the restored Royal Exhibition Building
Photographer: James Lauritz

Australian Society and Technology

Mr Nuttall's huge painting

On the morning of 9 May 1901, more than 12 000 people gathered in Melbourne's Exhibition Building to witness the opening of the first federal parliament. The event was the culmination of years of debate about the federation of the six Australian colonies. A new constitution had been approved by the people, and Australians were celebrating the birth of a new nation.

Among the crowd was Melbourne etcher and illustrator Charles Nuttall (1872–1934), who had been commissioned by a group of local businessmen to produce a large painting that would do justice to the day's significance.

Nuttall sketched furiously during the hour-long ceremony. Later, he set up a studio in the Exhibition Building. He travelled extensively to meet and draw many public figures: 344 people can be clearly identified in the work. His sponsors were delighted. The president of the Senate exclaimed that Australia's public men were 'as frequent in the picture as raisins in a plum pudding'.

Nuttall painted the moment when the sun streamed through the windows as the Duke of York declared parliament open. Prints of the painting, with a key, were presented to schools and libraries throughout Australia. Nuttall's painting, portraying the formality and the dignity of the occasion, became a popular and pervasive image of the beginning of the Australian nation. By publicising the personalities of the first Australian parliament, the painting gave them near-legendary status.

It had lost its popularity by 1930 and was stored in the damp basement of the Exhibition Building. As the centenary of Federation approached, it was 'rediscovered'. Restored in 1984, the painting came into the museum's collection in 1996. EW

Charles Nuttall, *The Opening of the First Federal Parliament, 9 May 1901* (1902), oil on canvas, H 226 × W 405 cm

Treasures of Museum Victoria

Shephard micro-ruling engine

This precision scientific instrument was made in Melbourne in the early 1890s by John Shephard, a Yorkshireman who immigrated in 1883. He became a founding partner in Davies, Shephard & Company of South Melbourne, specialising in the manufacture and repair of water meters, alongside general brass founding and engineering work.

Shephard was a keen member of the Field Naturalists' Club of Victoria, and it was through these amateur scientific interests that the company began making scientific instruments. By 1891 its advertisements offered sliding microtomes, used to prepare very thin slivers of specimens for viewing under a microscope. Subsequently, Shephard modified his microtome design to produce this precision micro-ruling engine, capable of cutting very fine, evenly spaced lines down to 0.5 micron (0.0005 millimetres) apart on a glass slide. His work helped set new international standards in the precision calibration of microscopes. MC

Weights and measures

Regulation of weights and measures was one of the first functions of governments everywhere; society depends upon accurate weights and measures for commerce, industry and science.

Weights and measures were regulated in Victoria from the earliest days of the colony. Checking weights and measures involves a physical comparison with a known standard. Thus the maintenance of primary standards and the production of authorised copies was an important task.

Primary standards were held initially by the Customs Board of Victoria, but the Melbourne Observatory produced authorised copies on the board's behalf. Between 1901 and 1945, the observatory, from where the pictured weights and measure come, was given oversight of the primary standards. When the observatory was closed in 1945, the Trade Measurement Branch was established and it occupied the observatory buildings for many years. MB

Detail of the micro-ruling engine (c. 1894), Davies, Shephard & Co., restoration by Ken Nuske of Monash University (1984),
H 25 x W 50 x D 25 cm

Imperial mass measures (c. 1865), Troughton & Simms
Detail of the standard yard (1915), W. & T. Avery

Australian Society and Technology

Regulator clock

This clock helped maintain standard time for Victoria from the 1860s until the 1920s. Government Astronomer Robert Ellery purchased the clock in 1865 from eminent London clock- and watchmaker Charles Frodsham, and installed it at the Melbourne Observatory. Fitted with platinum and gold electrical terminals, the clock could be linked electrically to recording devices and other clocks. Through careful nightly measurement of stars whose positions were accurately known, Ellery and his assistants established the longitude of the observatory and hence the precise time for Melbourne.

A precise time service and longitude measure enabled ships' captains to correct their chronometers, essential for safe navigation across large distances of ocean. At 1pm each day, a telegraphic signal from the observatory lowered a time ball on a bluestone tower at Williamstown, visible to ships anchored through Hobsons Bay.

Standard time flowed out from the observatory in a growing network. Telegraph connections were first made to the major public clocks in the city, at the post office, law courts, parliament and the railway stations. Then it gradually spread via the railways telegraph to every country town. Trains, workers, school children – all increasingly divided their days according to observatory time.

When Melbourne Observatory closed in 1945, the clock was transferred to Mount Stromlo Observatory in Canberra, and then sold in the 1990s to an overseas collector. An export licence was refused under the *Protection of Movable Cultural Heritage Act 1986*, which prevents the export of items of exceptional historical and cultural significance. The museum purchased the clock in 2001 with one of the first grants from the federal government's National Cultural Heritage Account and with contributions from the museum's Askew Bequest and the Royal Botanic Gardens (which now incorporates the former Melbourne Observatory buildings). RG

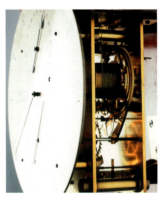

Charles Frodsham, regulator clock (1865), H 192 x W 43 x D 27 cm
The Williamstown time ball today, restored and protected as a significant heritage structure

Treasures of the Museum

Antarctic sledge

Ernest Shackleton's fame as an Antarctic explorer stems from the 1914–17 Transcontinental Expedition. On this voyage the ship was destroyed by pack ice, leaving the expeditioners to trek across the ice shelf and sail to an island off Antarctica. Yet not a single life was lost.

Shackleton's earlier expedition, in 1907–09, was equally important. It had its share of drama but also some lighter moments. On one occasion the motor car taken on the expedition overheated, leaving the explorers to wait in freezing conditions for it to cool down.

The aims of this expedition, like much Antarctic exploration, combined scientific curiosity with geopolitical interest. They included reaching the geographic South Pole and finding the Magnetic South Pole. Although Shackleton fell 100 miles (160 kilometres) short of the former goal, the latter was achieved when a party of three men, including Australian scientists Edgeworth David and Douglas Mawson, located the magnetic pole on 15 January 1909.

Other scientific highlights of the journey were the first ascent of Antarctica's only active volcano, Mount Erebus, and the discovery that some life forms in Antarctica can survive being completely frozen.

This sledge was used by Melburnian Bertram Armytage, who was in charge of the expedition's ponies. Although dogs eventually proved their worth in Antarctica, Shackleton's previous experience made him sceptical of their endurance. While this expedition did use some dogs – and a motorcar – Shackleton relied mainly on ponies to provide the hauling power for the expedition, with mixed success. MB

Alistair McKay, Edgeworth David and Douglas Mawson at the Magnetic South Pole
Source: South Australian Museum

Antarctic sledge (1907), H 20 x W 56 x L 341 cm

Australian Society and Technology

1–2

3–4

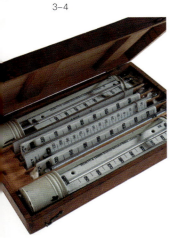

5–6

Objects from the Antarctic Collection

Surviving in the coldest, windiest continent on Earth is a perilous business. The average temperature is well below freezing, and strong blizzards are common.

Studying the weather of Antarctica has been an important scientific goal since the earliest days of exploration, and one that could help ensure an expedition's survival. These thermometers and barometer were used by Andrew Keith Jack on the western party of Shackleton's 1914–17 Transcontinental Expedition. Disaster struck this party when its ship was driven from shore before adequate supplies could be landed. The expeditioners spent two winters on minimal supplies before being rescued.

The role of clothing is vital. Early explorers used heavy clothing, which caused them to perspire. If the sweat froze, it could make them even colder. New materials developed in the 1940s and 1950s, and a greater appreciation of wind chill, led to the development of better protective clothing. The snowshoe and blizzard mask shown come from this later era. As well as the weather, long periods of darkness and isolation can be treacherous. Recreational pursuits, such as music, are important in countering this. The piano accordion also dates from the postwar era, when Australia established a permanent presence on Antarctica.

Today, scientific research is the primary activity in Antarctica, recently joined by tourism. The thrill of exploration of a continent largely unknown remains strong. This half sledge was used by Greg Mortimer on the first ascent of Mount Minto in North Victoria Land in 1987. MB

1   Blizzard mask (c. 1950), W 28 x L 46 cm
2   Barometer (c. 1910), diam. 8.5 x cm
3   Snow shoe (1950), W 39 x L 109 cm
4   Half sledge (1988), H 35 x W 70 x L 166 cm
5   Thermometers in original case (c.1910), W 35 x D 6.5 cm
6   Piano accordion (1940–50), H23 x W 23 x D 48 cm

Treasures of the Museum

Geodetic survey of Victoria

Surveying was a major undertaking in the new colony of Victoria. It provided the grid by which land was appropriated by the colonial government and parcelled out for farming, mining, townships, roads and railways. But the work of hordes of contract surveyors had to be related to fixed survey points to avoid confusion and overlapping titles. In 1858, Surveyor-General Charles Ligar appointed Government Astronomer Robert Ellery to undertake a geodetic survey of Victoria.

It was a huge task that took 13 years to complete. Selected stars were observed repeatedly at Williamstown and later Melbourne Observatory so that their precise positions were known; surveyors in the field would observe the same stars to accurately determine their location. A baseline eight miles (13 kilometres) long was measured near Werribee, on the 145th meridian of longitude. This required painstaking measurement using three 10-foot (three-metre) measuring rods, adjusting carefully for temperature changes and undulations in the terrain.

Field parties of surveyors, armed with telescopes and portable altazimuth instruments (large and highly accurate theodolites), then built up a series of mathematical triangles across Victoria, from the original Werribee baseline, installing markers on mountains and prominent landmarks along the boundaries of the colony. It was often hard going – a mixture of demanding physical labour and precise measurement. In Gippsland, surveyors had to bash through thick scrub and clear gaps on the hills from which they could use heliotropes to reflect the sun's rays to the next surveying party. RG

Head of the geodetic survey post
Altazimuth (1836), Troughton & Simms, H 105 x W 52 x D 80 cm
Geodetic survey post (1867), installed near Shepparton, central Victoria, H 170 x W 30 x D 26 cm

Australian Society and Technology

Sunshine Stripper Harvester

Frustrated by the slow and laborious nature of harvesting wheat, Hugh Victor McKay, at the age of 18, assembled a stripper harvester on his father's property at Drummarton, Victoria, in 1884. While a number of similar machines had been developed, the popularity of the Sunshine Stripper Harvester was able to secure McKay's place as one of the most successful agricultural implement makers in Australia.

The harvester played an important role in establishing Australia as a leading cereal producing country, and it was one of the first manufactured products to be exported. The H.V. McKay Company also manufactured an extensive range of other farming equipment and implements. By the 1920s it had become the largest manufacturing enterprise in the Southern Hemisphere, employing more than 3000 workers.

The McKay Collection is regarded as one of the most significant industrial heritage collections in Australia. It began with donations from Hugh Victor McKay in the first decade of the 20th century, and a number of important family donations were made during the 1960s. The largest donation came as the result of an employee rescuing material from a rubbish skip in the 1980s.

The collection ranges from the 1880s to the most recent agricultural developments. It features more than 13 000 photographs, 750 films, more than 3000 trade publications, working models of equipment, a rare Sunshine model 'A' tractor, company archives and the original blacksmith shop where the first stripper harvester was made. LDH

Cover of H.V. McKay Co. trade catalogue (c. 1906)
Sunshine Stripper Harvester (c. 1906), H.V. McKay Co., H 230 x W 280 x L 340 cm

Barbed wire

Condemned by some as 'devil's rope' for causing injury to livestock, barbed wire offered Australian settlers a cheap, portable and practical form of fencing. This simple technology has significance beyond its original use in agriculture. It has played a central role in the settlement and occupation of land, the incarceration of people, the harnessing of nature and as a tool of mass warfare. Barbed wire has also been used for creating music, and as a symbol of popular culture and political expression.

The Jack Chisholm Collection has more than 1400 fencing wire samples, from the first 1870s patents to modern razor wire.

With more than 530 patented barbed wires, approximately 2000 variations, and more than 2000 patented barbed-wire tools, barbed wire has become popular with collectors. LDH

A selection of barbed wire from the museum's collection (1870s–1943)

Stump jump plough

Mallee scrublands were transformed by the world's first stump jump plough, invented in 1876 by Richard B. Smith and his brother, Clarence, in Kalkabury, South Australia. The stump jump mechanism lifted the ploughshare over roots, stones and other obstacles in the soil, thereby avoiding damage to horses and equipment, and giving farmers a living during the slow process of land clearing. Originally criticised as a 'slovenly' way of farming, the plough soon became the single most important tool in 'taming' Australian mallee scrublands.

The stump jump principle was adopted across the world to almost the whole range of tillage, seeding and fertiliser implements. Australia's leading agricultural implement company, H.V. McKay Company, successfully used this principle in their ploughs and other implements, and was the manufacturer of this model. LDH

Stump jump plough model (early 20th century), H.V. McKay Co., H 25.5 x W 29 x L 61.5 cm

Australian Society and Technology

Cowley steam traction engine

The Cowley steam traction engine, acquired by the museum in 1985, is one of the most significant relics of Australia's age of steam. As one of only two surviving Australian-built traction engines, it represents a landmark in Victoria's early engineering development.

Built by Cowley's Eureka Ironworks at Ballarat in 1916, the engine was based largely on a standard British design, but incorporated significant local innovations in both the firebox and road wheels.

Restoration of the Cowley traction engine by the museum was a major project, involving a team of 30 staff and volunteers in some 5000 hours of work over a 16-year period. Today the engine can be seen in operation in all its former splendour as part of the Working Machinery Program at Scienceworks. MC

PMA safety hood

This yellow hood, heavily stained with pigment, is one of hundreds of pieces of safety gear and other items collected from Pigment Manufacturers of Australia Ltd (PMA) upon its closure in 1991. Operating for 30 years in Laverton in Melbourne's west, PMA produced red, yellow, green and blue pigments for the paint, printing and plastic industries. For the 90 workers across two plants, it was hot, noisy, dirty and dangerous work. Roy Dyer, a PMA maintenance worker in the 1980s, recalls the discomfort of the safety gear: 'It was always 40 degrees . . . and you had this bloody PVC stuff on. No wonder I was as skinny as a rake'. MMcC

Single-cylinder, six nominal horsepower steam traction engine (1916), Cowley's Eureka Ironworks Pty Ltd, H 322.5 x W 251.5 x L 579 cm

Safety hood (mid-1980s), L 93 x W 45 cm

Phillip Adams

The most famous quadruped in Australia

When I was a kid I would beg to be taken to either Luna Park or the museum. While thrilled by the centrifugal delights of the St Kilda fairground, I preferred the gloomy, echoing precincts of the museum. Though lacking the ambrosial smells of fairy floss and waffle, it provided a more profound experience, and it was far more mysterious and confronting than the 'Boo!' of the ghost train.

The museum had made an effort, in the dawn of the 'interactive display', to capture the attention and index fingers of the child. You could press a button and watch an old donkey engine go through a few circular motions. Yet the displays that *didn't* move, that were unnaturally and alarmingly still, were the most enthralling. There were stuffed gorillas that an early museum director had brought to Australia in the hope of ridiculing the evolutionary theories of Darwin. And nearby were the dioramas of Aboriginal life, wherein life-sized effigies of Indigenous people cooked kangaroos and posed with spears. But the exhibit I found most exciting of all was a stuffed horse.

I grew up on a little flower farm in East Kew, and we had a horse, a giant called Blossom that my grandfather used for ploughing. Thus I was on intimate terms with an even bigger horse than Phar Lap. Yet there was something about Phar Lap's stance, intensified by his motionlessness, which was riveting. I marvelled at the way his veins and ligaments were as vividly preserved as his hide. And what about the eye? Was it real? There were many nose prints on the glass case. Not only those of little boys but of grown men. Next to Simpson's donkey, Phar Lap was the most famous quadruped in Australia.

This was not one of your Madame Tussaud experiences where you would quibble over the accuracy of the representation. Behold the real thing. The horse

that more Australians had cheered more loudly than any other. The horse that had carried much more than the most famous jockeys. It carried, we were reminded constantly, 'the emotions of a nation'. And it expressed the sense of loss that characterised Australian history. The tragedy, the defeat that gave us so much of our national mythology. We wrote our history in the blood of the fallen at Gallipoli, in the failures of Burke and Wills, and of Lassiter to find his lost reef. In the defeats of brave pioneers confronted by a brutally indifferent nature that wiped them out with drought, flood and bushfire.

And Phar Lap embodied another idea – that of being done in by our enemies. Phar Lap was a story of betrayal, like that of Les Darcy. He was not just a horse he was a four-legged messiah who had died a redemptive death.

My name, Phillip, means 'lover of horses'. Apart from Phar Lap, and Blossom, it has never been true. These days I live on a cattle property with horses galore, but while they are immensely useful I don't respond to them with particular emotion. In that glass case, however, was one of my most enduring heroes – which is odd, given that I have never been to a race meeting and never placed a bet.

Phillip Adams, AO, is an architect of the modern Australian film industry and producer of such classics as 'Barry McKenzie', 'Don's Party' and 'The Getting of Wisdom'. He has been a controversial newspaper columnist for half a century, and his influential radio program, 'Late Night Live', is heard around Australia on Radio National and across the world on Radio Australia.

Phar Lap on display at the museum
Phar Lap's convincing win at the Melbourne Cup, 4 November 1930
Museum Victoria Collection

Attractions in an extraordinary bookshop

Edward W. Cole arrived in Victoria in 1852, seeking gold. Although unsuccessful he remained undaunted, and attempted many different ventures before turning to bookselling. In 1883, he opened his successful Coles Book Arcade, located in Bourke Street between Swanston and Elizabeth streets. Selling new and second-hand books, Cole encouraged his customers to spend time in his shop by introducing a variety of attractions, including a band, a confectionery department, caged monkeys and parrots, a fernery, redeemable medals, a clockwork symphonion, clockwork hens and 'Little Men' – sometimes known as 'Little Sailors'.

The symphonion, in its ornately carved wooden case, was an early form of mechanical music box. To play a tune, customers inserted a coin or token, causing the steel disc to rotate. Small hooks on the back of the disc plucked the teeth of a metal comb. Discs providing different tunes were stored in the lower cupboard.

An advertisement for a mechanical hen was enclosed with the symphonion when it arrived from Germany. Cole subsequently purchased five or six hens and numerous eggs. On insertion of the appropriate coin, the hen would cackle and lay a tin egg containing a sweet or small toy. The eggs were re-used.

The 'Little Men' were manufactured in Melbourne for one of Cole's earlier bookshops. They sat in the front window and turned a double crank handle powered by water pressure. The handle turned tin advertising signs promoting books and departments, and slogans reflecting Cole's attitude to religion and morality. AM

Symphonion (c. 1889), H 215 x W 83.4 x D 48 cm
Mechanical hen (c. 1889), H64 x W 35 X L 50 cm
One of Cole's 'Little Men' (1883), F. Ziegler & Sons

Australian Society and Technology

Le Forgeron Marionettes

On 11 May 1935, Melbourne's *Argus* newspaper published a piece about a local theatre company of '150 actors who sleep in a storeroom'. Almost 70 years later, and 50 years after their last performance, the same group awoke and made the journey to the museum. They are the puppets from Le Forgeron Marionettes, made and operated by a Melbourne family from the 1920s until 1956, including a residency at a purpose-built theatre in St Kilda's landmark Luna Park.

Scottish-born cabinet-maker Alex Smith took up puppetry as a hobby when he was a boy. Later, after performing in London, he moved his family to Melbourne in 1927, where his hobby became a full-time occupation. He and his wife and son made the marionettes, dressed them, constructed the sets, wrote the scripts and carried out the onstage and backstage functions needed to perform the plays. As well as performing in its permanent theatre, the company appeared at department stores, schools, town halls, church functions, private parties and various charity events.

The collection arrived at the museum with a small archive of newspaper clippings, programs, scripts and other documents, which gives an intriguing insight into the history and operation of Le Forgeron Marionettes. The clowns, bears, pirates, penguins, soldiers, kings and queens, monkeys and various other characters now have a permanent home, and will again be enjoyed by the people of Melbourne. MR

Spanish dancer (c. 1930), H 52 x W 14 cm
Sultan (c. 1930), H 62 x W 15 cm
Courtesy of Kaye and Murray Smith

No 1 cable tram

On Monday 11 November 1885, the No 1 cable tram inaugurated Melbourne's first tram service, running along Bridge Road, Richmond, and Flinders Street, terminating at Spencer Street. It was the beginning of a new era in public transport. By 1891, Melbourne had built one of the world's largest cable-tramway networks, with 17 routes extending over 75 kilometres of track and powered by large steam engines in 12 coal-fired engine houses.

The No 1 cable tram was one of 20 tramcar sets imported from New York. Later sets were built in Melbourne to a similar design. Each cable tram set consisted of a 'dummy' engine or grip car, with open bench seating and an enclosed trailer or saloon car, where women and non-smoking passengers could sit out of the weather.

The system was operated by continuously moving steel cables that ran in tunnels beneath the tracks. A grip mechanism from the dummy car extended through a slot in the centre of set of tracks to engage the cable.

The No 1 cable tram made its final run on 30 June 1927, when the Richmond route closed for conversion to electric trams. In 1940, following the closure of the final cable route, the No 1 tram set was donated by the Melbourne & Metropolitan Tramways Board to the Historical Collection of the Public Library. It spent the next 24 years gathering dust under a corrugated-iron lean-to against the southern wall of the museum's Swanston Street site. In 1974, the No 1 tram was finally restored at the Preston Tramway Workshops and installed in its own purpose-built, glazed display building on the corner of Russell and Little Lonsdale streets. MC

The first day of operation on the Richmond route, showing the amazing capacity of the robust little cable tramcars
Museum Victoria Collection

Details of the No 1 cable tram 'dummy' car (1885), John Stephenson & Co., H 316 x W 230 x L 490 cm

Australian Society and Technology

Thomson steam car

When the young Melbourne engineer Herbert Thomson began designing and constructing his first steam car in 1896, he had never seen an automobile, and the term 'motor car' was yet to find its way into everyday language. He called his invention a 'steam phaeton' after the style of the horsedrawn vehicle on which it was modelled.

By 1898, Thomson was making the first road trials of his steam car, but he did not seek public recognition until after lodging a provisional patent in June 1899. Shortly afterwards, assisted by his cousin Edward Holmes, he formed Thomson Motor Car Ltd with the ambition of becoming Australia's first motor car manufacturer.

In April 1900, Thomson and Holmes took the prototype car by steamship to Sydney and exhibited it at the Royal Easter and Bathurst shows, before embarking on an ambitious 790-kilometre overland journey, driving from Bathurst back to Melbourne. The event rates as the first significant interstate motor car trip in Australia, and as an inspired publicity stunt was an outstanding success. Within six months the company had received orders or inquiries for £10 000 worth of cars. It went on to produce about 10 more steam cars to an improved design over the next three years, before succumbing to the pressures of limited capital, delivery delays and quality problems with imported and locally made components, and competition from imported motor vehicles.

Following the inventor's death in 1947, the original Thomson steam car was restored by Mr W.A. Buchanan and donated to the museum in 1960 by the inventor's daughter. MC

Herbert Thomson demonstrates his steam 'phaeton' at the Bendigo Show, 1899
Museum Victoria Collection

Steam car (c. 1898), Herbert Thomson,
H 178 x W 142 x L 271 cm
Photographer: David Loram, DDL Photographics

65

Treasures of Museum Victoria

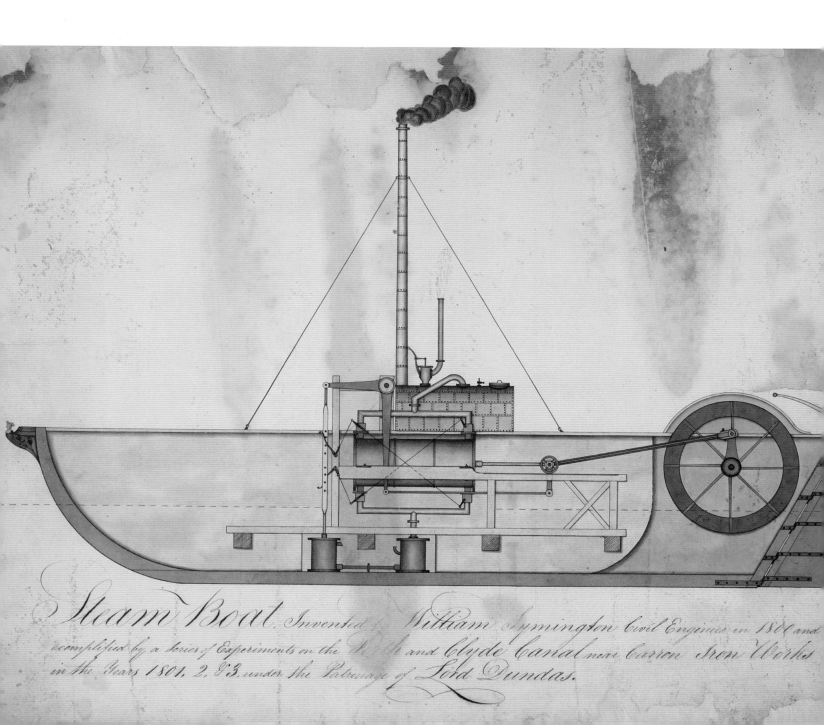

Australian Society and Technology

The Charlotte Dundas model and drawings

Among the museum's water transport collection is a group of artefacts with a direct connection to William Symington, popularly known as 'the father of steam navigation'. Symington was born in the Scottish mining village of Leadhills in 1763, and by his 20s had acquired a reputation as a mechanical engineer and designer of atmospheric steam engines for mines and factories. His early interest in steamboats began in 1787, when he was commissioned to build a small pleasure steamer for trial on Loch Dalswinton. It was not until 1803, however, that his fourth and final paddle-steamer, the *Charlotte Dundas*, underwent a successful public trial, towing two heavily laden barges on an historic 30-kilometre journey along the Forth and Clyde Canal linking Edinburgh and Glasgow. This event is now recognised as one of the first practical demonstrations of steam-powered navigation, even though the Canal Company failed to subsequently commercialise the invention.

The museum holds the oldest surviving model of the *Charlotte Dundas*, made in 1852 by Andrew Symington, the inventor's eldest son. The model was brought to Australia when another son, William, immigrated in 1855, and it was exhibited at both the 1866 and 1888 exhibitions in Melbourne.

Other objects connected to Symington include a plaster bust of the inventor, made after his death in 1831, and a series of eight superb hand-coloured engineering drawings. Three of these are original 1785 drawings showing details of James Watt's design for the Wanlockhead Pumping Engine on which Symington began his career. The other drawings, done by William Symington himself, show otherwise unrecorded details of his early steamboat designs and other inventions. MC

William Symington, section drawing of the *Charlotte Dundas* (c. 1827), H 43.5 x W 56 cm

Andrew Symington, model of the *Charlotte Dundas* (1852), H 35.2 x W 20 x L 76.2 cm

Treasures of the Museum

Concord coach

The Concord thorough brace coach is one of the oldest objects in the museum's transport collections. Built by Abbott & Downing of Concord, New Hampshire, USA, in 1869, the coach is of the same make and style as the first American coaches Freeman Cobb & Co. introduced on Victorian goldfields routes in 1854.

This coach was imported by another American, Francis Boardman Clapp, who had earlier founded a coach line in western Victoria. Clapp was also the Melbourne agent for Abbott & Downing and was involved with other Victorian transport enterprises, including the Melbourne Omnibus Company and the Melbourne Tramway & Omnibus Company, which later operated Melbourne's cable-tram network.

The museum's Concord coach spent the later part of its working life with Aisbett's Royal Mail Line and Vines & McPhee in the goldfields district south-west of Ballarat. There it carried passengers and mail from the railway station at Scarsdale to the mining settlements at Pitfield and Berringa. Remarkably, the coach remained in service until 1924, an exceptional record for a vehicle that spent most of its life on rough, unmade roads. The coach could carry up to 20 passengers at a time and would typically have been drawn by five horses, which were replaced at 'stages' every few kilometres.

Today, the coach is of international significance, being one of the few surviving Concord coaches remaining unrestored in its last working condition. MC

Aisbett's Concord coach on its last outing as a working coach, outside the Melbourne *Argus* office during Victoria's centenary celebrations in 1934
Museum Victoria Collection

Aisbett's Concord coach (c. 1869), Abbot, Downing & Co., H 330 x W 210 x L 430 cm

Australian Society and Technology

Skyline caravan

Vinyl car seats sticky with sweat and gritty with sand; tripping over guy ropes while weaving between camp sites; the hiss of the gas light; and the smell of fresh fish cooking on small stoves – memories of the great Aussie holiday.

In 1957, Richard and Jean Hayes paid £183 for a modest cream-coloured caravan with a mint-green roof and black trim from Skyline Caravans in Caulfield, Melbourne. Over the years, the couple and their four children stayed at caravan parks throughout eastern Australia every Christmas holidays. The caravan is typical of its era and, apart from a repaint (in similar colours) in the 1970s, blinkers and brake lights, and new curtains, all the features are original, down to the metal-lined ice chest and the bread bin. The family donated other objects with the caravan, including the annexe, poles, guy ropes and tent pegs; picnic crockery, cutlery and Primus stove; saucepan, toaster and a folding chair.

Over the years, the caravan was towed first by a Vanguard, then an HR Holden and finally a Holden Torana. The family recall the excitement of packing the van, setting the alarm clock and leaving early while it was still dark, as well as the amused looks of fellow travellers as they glanced from the tiny van to the car full of people. The Skyline was cramped, cosy, simple and exciting – a story that resonates with any Australian family who has ever packed up the van, the kids, the car and headed for the highway. MMcF

Caravan (1957), plywood, Skyline Caravans,
H 230.8 x W 210.5 x L 390.4 cm

Oppermann's racing bicycles

Hubert Opperman was a cherished Australian sporting hero of the 1920s and 1930s whose cycling achievements inspired millions during the Depression.

In 1922, as a relatively unknown 17 year old, Opperman achieved his first success with a third place in the gruelling Cycle Traders 100-mile (160-kilometre) road race, winning a new £10 Malvern Star sports bike. Thus began an association with Malvern Star that lasted half a lifetime and helped shape the destiny of both Opperman and the company he came to represent. Over the next two decades, 'Oppy' went on to win more than 50 major road races and hundreds of track events in Australia, England and Europe, establishing dozens of world records in the process.

In 1931, Oppy donated to the museum the bicycles on which he had achieved two of his most significant world records. MC

Left: Malvern Star 'Tour de France' racer ridden by Hubert Opperman in his 24-hour unpaced road distance world record between Mount Gambier and Melbourne in 1927, H 100 x L 180 cm; Right: Malvern Star modified bicycle ridden by Hubert Opperman in his 24-hour motor-paced distance record at the Melbourne Motodrome in April 1930, H 85 x L 154 cm

A selection of the 150 cycling trophies, sashes, medals and certificates won by Hubert Opperman between 1922 and 1938

Australian Society and Technology

Burston's 'Victory' high-wheel bicycle

This Victory penny farthing bicycle, assembled by H. Bassett & Company of Melbourne, is perhaps the most travelled bicycle in the museum's collection. Built as a special order for the keen Melbourne cyclist George W. Burston, it is a typical high-wheel or 'ordinary' bicycle of the style popular in the 1880s, with a 56-inch (142-centimetre) diameter front wheel and solid rubber tyres.

On 1 November 1889, Burston set off on this bicycle on a 'world tour', accompanied by Harry Stokes, a fellow member of the Melbourne Cycling Club, riding a similar machine. Making first for Sydney, they then boarded a steamer to Brisbane and Batavia (now Indonesia). Continuing through India, the Middle East, Europe and the United Kingdom they covered 10 000 kilometres by bicycle over the next 10 months on a journey through more than 15 countries. MC

'Victory' brand high-wheel touring bicycle (1889),
H. Bassett & Co., H 161 x L 168 cm

Duigan biplane

When John Robertson Duigan wrote to the Industrial and Technological Museum in 1920, offering to donate an aircraft he had built 'many years ago about 1910', the curator, R.H. Walcott, immediately recognised a unique piece of Australian aviation heritage; it was the 'first Australian-made aircraft to fly'.

Duigan was born at Terang, Victoria, in 1882, and studied electrical and motor engineering in London, before returning to Victoria to join his younger brother, Reginald, managing a family property at Mia Mia near Heathcote. Inspired by the achievements of the Wright brothers in the United States, he built a glider in 1908 and managed to fly it in a strong wind tethered to 110 metres of fencing wire.

Following this success, Duigan began work on a powered aircraft, which he first flew on 16 July 1910. Over succeeding months, further modifications and improvements were made until he managed sustained flights of up to a kilometre at heights of 30 metres. In January 1911, Duigan demonstrated his plane to newspaper reporters, and the following April he made several public flights before a crowd of 1000 at the Bendigo Racecourse.

Duigan's achievement is all the more remarkable for the fact that he had never seen or flown an aircraft previously and had little technical information with which to work. His first design was based on little more than a postcard of the Wright Flyer. With the exception of the engine and propeller, every component was made by Duigan and his brother in a rudimentary workshop on the farm. MC

John Duigan makes an early test flight at 'Spring Plains' Station, Mia Mia, in 1910
Museum Victoria Collection
Detail of the Duigan biplane (1910), H 295 x W 730 x L 1100 cm

Australian Society and Technology

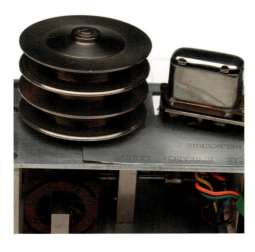

Black box flight recorder

A series of unexplained crashes by the world's first passenger jet aircraft in the early 1950s led Melbourne scientist Dr David Warren to invent the device now known as the black box flight recorder.

After seeing a miniature German-made dictaphone that recorded sounds on a fine steel wire, Dr Warren convinced the government's Aeronautical Research Laboratories to adapt the concept into a practical prototype known as 'Flight Memory'. Tests showed that a wire recording could withstand the high temperatures and impact of an aircraft crash and subsequent fire, and could be used to recover cockpit voices and in-flight aircraft instrument data that might help crash investigators.

Despite its potential, Australian authorities were initially uninterested and it was left to overseas companies to commercialise the invention. Today, all civilian aircraft worldwide carry black box flight recorders, which ironically are painted fluorescent orange to enable them to be more easily found among crash site wreckage. MC

Detail of the 'Flight Memory' voice and cockpit data recorder (c. 1956), Aeronautical Research Laboratories, H 7.8 x W 6.5 x L 15.8 cm

Fireproof case used for testing the 'Flight Memory' prototype recorder (c. 1956), Aeronautical Research Laboratories, H 19.5 x W 19.5 x L 26 cm

The Commonwealth Aircraft Corporation's Deliverette

One of the cutest and most unusual vehicles in the museum's transport collection is the small, aluminium-bodied motor van known as the Deliverette. Conceived and built by the Commonwealth Aircraft Corporation (CAC) in Melbourne, in the late 1940s, the Deliverette was designed as a prototype lightweight delivery van.

The innovative design was powered by a twin-cylinder BMW motorcycle engine, with front-wheel drive. Folding side doors and controls that could be operated while standing were designed for ease of use by drivers continually stopping and alighting to make deliveries.

The project was devised to utilise the design skills, workforce and manufacturing technology developed by CAC through the production of 1200 aircraft for the RAAF during the Second World War. Although tests of the prototype proved successful, the project was later abandoned when the company won contracts to build engines for the RAAF's first jet fighters and to develop a new trainer and advanced jet fighter. MC

Deliverette (1947), Commonwealth Aircraft Corporation, H 228 x W 162 x L 396 cm

Harry Johns' boxing truck

Harry Johns was a boxing and wrestling entrepreneur who toured the agricultural shows of Australia's eastern states between the 1930s and 1960s. This vehicle reflects his lengthy involvement in the business. The cabin and chassis, from the International AR 160 Series, were purchased new by Johns around 1954; the rear section was grafted from his previous truck.

The vehicle blends social and technological significance on a national scale. Travelling boxing troupes can be traced to the late 1800s, but it was not until road transport improved that troupes became a regular feature of country shows. Instead of relying on rail and local transport, Johns' troupe could travel direct from show to show, his truck a travelling advertisement carrying several tons of set-up equipment. This included the tent in which the boxing was staged; a drum and a sound system so that the spruiker Johns could drown out the showground competition; a 'line-up board' on which a dozen fighters would be paraded and matched with local hopefuls ('C'mon – who'll take a glove, who'll take a glove?'); and the general supplies of a life lived rough. On top of all this travelled the fighters themselves. Many were recruited along the way after showing promise against a Johns fighter. At least half of these fighters were Aboriginal men as tent boxing was one of the only ways a young man could break out from 'the Mission'.

Dong! With a fight in progress the tent was an arena of race, class and gender tensions. Those who watched the fights recall the sheer excitement and the funk of sweat, beer and cheap perfume. EBB

International AR 160 series truck (c. 1953) restored to how it would have looked when the show ended in 1969

Australian Society and Technology

Fawkner printing press

The *Melbourne Advertiser*, the first Melbourne newspaper, was printed on this press in 1838. The publisher, John Pascoe Fawkner, was an entrepreneur taking advantage of opportunities presented by the young colony of Victoria. In a competitive climate, he was anxious to be the first to establish a newspaper. Fawkner obtained the press just before the production of the 10th edition. In his haste to publish, previous editions of his paper had been handwritten. The press, believed to date from the first half of the 18th century, was replaced with a more efficient model in 1840. DD

Statue of Mercury

When the four-metre statue of *Mercury* was placed at the top of the *Age* building in Collins Street in 1899, people were assured the statue could not fall. It was held in place by a steel tube fixed three metres into the wall.

The *Age* itself was launched in 1854, the same year as the founding of the museum. Victoria's gold rush had begun, and the colony was teaming with people seeking their fortunes. *Mercury* was an appropriate symbol to represent the newspaper's role in communication: he was the messenger of the Roman gods. DD

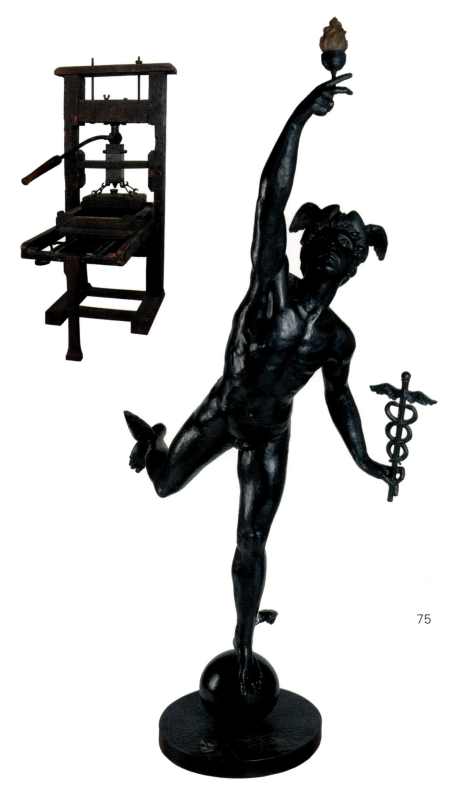

Fawkner printing press (early 18th century), H 193 x W 148 x D 78 cm
Charles Richardson, *Mercury* (1899), cast by W. Rooke, H 348 x W 185 x D 100 cm

Detail of ceremonial headdress (see page 127)

Indigenous Cultures

Treasures of the Museum

Wurundjeri pencil sketch

The 19th-century Aboriginal artist who signed this drawing 'Timothy, Coranderrk' (c. 1830–75) was recorded as 'Koorook-koonong' in the census of residents at Coranderrk Aboriginal Station at Healesville in 1863. Annotations to a photographic portrait taken by Charles Walter a few years later recorded Timothy's name as 'Gurruk-coonim aged 34 years' and 'Son of the King (of the Yarra Tribe) and himself a King'. The portraits from Coranderrk taken by Walter were exhibited in the 1866 Intercolonial Exhibition in Melbourne.

The artist belonged to the Wurundjeri clan whose territory is marked by the Yarra River. The undated pencil sketch is the only known work by this artist, and would have been done between 1863 and 1875. It could be either two separate drawings or a single work on two sheets of paper. Like the sketches by 19th-century artist Tommy McRae, Timothy has drawn hunting scenes, including a party of men with a dog trying to catch kangaroos. The panel on the lower right has bearded men similar to those depicted in corroboree paintings by William Barak.

The drawing is likely to predate the works of McRae and Barak, and the artist has possibly included himself in the work. The photographic portrait bears a striking resemblance to the small kneeling figure to the left of the signature. The bearded man sits at the edge of a group of 10 men with spears upright and five women with children holding digging sticks. The most extraordinary element is the top panel, which appears to depict an eclipse or other lunar phenomenon. LA

Timothy at Coranderrk (c. 1865), albumen print
Photographer: Charles Walter, Museum Victoria Collection

Timothy, untitled (n.d.), pencil on paper, H 75 x W 52 cm

Indigenous Cultures

Rutherglen Corroboree

This drawing was posted to the director of the National Museum of Victoria with 'Presented by Mrs A. Pattenden 15.7.29' written in ink on the sketch. The accompanying letter from Mrs Pattenden suggested the director discard the work if it was of no interest. Nearly 70 years later, the sketch and the letter were recovered in the original envelope when the museum's library was being packed for relocation to the site at Carlton Gardens.

The distinctive pen and ink drawing of silhouetted dancing corroboree figures is typical of the work of the 19th-century Aboriginal artist Tommy McRae (c. 1830–1901). The body of each man is illustrated with distinctive and individual ceremonial designs. McRae was perhaps the first published Aboriginal artist in Australia; sketches from the museum and the State Library of Victoria collections were included in the 1929 *Primitive Art* exhibition. Little credit was given to McRae's artistic skill in the exhibition catalogue, which described his work as 'showing European influence'. It is possible that Mrs Pattenden saw the exhibition and consequently donated this work.

McRae gained recognition for his work in his lifetime and sold drawings for cash and commissions. He was known variously as Tommy McCrae, Tommy Barnes, Yakaduna and Chief of the Wahgunyah tribe of north-eastern Victoria. McRae began sketching in the 1860s, and much of the subject matter for his works was drawn from memory and oral traditions. He mostly used black ink, but sometimes worked with red, blue and purple. McRae began by drawing the ground and then working the figures upwards. LA

Tommy McRae, *Rutherglen Corroboree* (1899), pencil and ink on paper, H 27.5 x W 33 cm

80

Carol Cooper

South-eastern shields

Intricate designs in wood characterise the visual culture of south-eastern Australian Aboriginal people in the 19th century. The shields shown here demonstrate the major types, which include the narrow, wedge or elliptical-shaped shields for parrying the blows of hardwood clubs, and the broad shields with handles either carved from the solid wood or made from cane inserted into central holes.

While some shields might have been collected by the victors of battle, like that pictured second from the top left – 'taken in a fight between the Native Police and the Avoca Tribe at Creswick's Waterhole, July 1847' – others found their way into collections by being traded or purchased. The names of the makers or owners of those shields remain unknown.

One of the most striking shields is third from the bottom left. This broad shield was collected by William Le Souëf, one of the early Aboriginal Protectors, from the Murchison Aboriginal Station on the Goulburn River in the 1840s. It shows a typical south-eastern design, with rows of recessed and ochred diamond motifs enclosed by herringbone patterns infilled with white pipe clay.

The meticulous carving with stone and animal-tooth engravers was combined with ochres and clays to produce designs both visually arresting and distracting. They had the power to create optical illusions during battle, a quality enhanced by the dexterity of the warriors.

The designs on the shields were infinitely variable, and no two are exactly the same. Like other art forms in the south-east, the meaning of the designs is thought to relate to individual and group identity. Shields were also viewed as having innate power, and an old shield that had 'won many fights' was prized as an object of trade.

Shields (1850–1900), natural pigments on wood, H 66–133 x W 7.5–28.5 cm

Carol Cooper
Possum-skin cloak

This magnificent possum-skin cloak was obtained in 1872 from a member of the Gunditjmara community living on the Anglican Aboriginal Mission Station at Lake Condah, in Victoria's Western District. It is made from the pelts of 50 Brush-tailed Possums, carefully sewn together with kangaroo sinew and made pliable by elaborate incised linear designs highlighted with red ochre.

Contemporary accounts and drawings suggest that Aboriginal people in the south-east commonly wore cloaks for warmth and status. The cloak's collector, R.E. Johns, thought it to be 'of genuine native design', and a good example of those worn before colonisation. Its abstract motifs are similar to those engraved on weapons or on burial trees and were connected to the identity of the wearer.

Cloak (1872), natural pigments on possum skin, L 160 x W 220 cm

Carol Cooper

Bungaleen's grave marker

The memorial for Thomas Bungaleen (1847–65), made at Coranderrk Aboriginal Station in 1866, is a rare example of Aboriginal woodcarving. The artist was probably Simon Wonga, the headman of the Wurundjeri people, who inhabited the land around Melbourne.

The story of the carving has been interpreted to represent an inquiry into Bungaleen's death. The upper figures carrying spears are the investigators. The cluster of animals indicates that he had not starved, while the strange forms below were said to be the spirits who caused his death by 'their wicked enchantements [sic]'.

Thomas Bungaleen was the son of a Gippsland headman whose family was brought to Melbourne by the Native Police in 1847. After his father's death, the boy was placed in the Merri Creek Aboriginal School under the supervision of Assistant Protector of Aborigines William Thomas. In 1861, Bungaleen was bonded to work on the steamship *Victoria*, where he won approval following a trip to the northern coast in search of the missing Burke and Wills Expedition. Bungaleen died in 1865 and was buried in the Melbourne Cemetery.

The style of incised decoration on Bungaleen's memorial is similar to the distinctive linear designs featured on south-eastern carved shields and on possum-skin cloaks. The layering and figurative elements of the composition are also linked to the beautiful ochre and watercolour drawings of renowned Coranderrk artist William Barak, who became the Wurundjeri headman after Wonga's death.

Carol Cooper is Manager of Registration at the National Museum of Australia, Canberra. She has been a curator for several important exhibitions and has undertaken major research on overseas collections of Aboriginal and Torres Strait Islander objects.

Grave marker (1860s), natural pigments on carved wood, H 130 x W 35 cm

Treasures of the Museum

Carved human figure

This rare surviving example of sculpture from Aboriginal Victoria was made by Bullock Jack, who lived at Ramahyuck Mission Station in Gippsland in the 19th century. The effigy, made of wood with remnants of white ochre remaining on its surface, is almost a metre tall. One report suggests it was modelled on figures made for sacred ceremonies. The historical image shows a similar effigy displayed beside boomerangs on the home of Bullock Jack. Details of the artist's life are not known.

The only other surviving sculptural forms from Victoria are several bark drawings from the Loddon River area, which are held in British institutions. This effigy was donated to the museum in 1974 by Miss R.L. Hagenauer. GS

Sculptures on the hut of Bullock Jack, late 19th century
Museum Victoria Collection

Bullock Jack, human figure (19th century), natural pigment on wood, H 910 x W 390 cm

Indigenous Cultures

Bark canoe

This is the only remaining 19th-century Aboriginal canoe from the Melbourne region. Scottish immigrant John Buchan collected the canoe in the 1850s from local Aborigines camping near his home overlooking the Yarra River at Studley Park. The site where the Merri Creek joins the Yarra, upstream from Buchan's Kew home, was a traditional camping ground and ceremonial site. The river flats and lagoons of the Yarra River were favoured places for the Wurundjeri people, providing a plentiful supply of fish, eels and birds' eggs. Canoes provided an easy means of travelling through the lagoons and into reed beds.

This canoe carries evidence that it was made after European arrival. There are several sharp cuts in the edge of the bark that have been made by a metal axe.

Three types of rope have been used to tie the canoe into shape; two of these are handmade, but the third is machine-made European twine. Most striking are the three metal straps (taken from a wooden barrel) that maintain the canoe's shape; we shall never know if the Wurundjeri makers incorporated the bands into their traditional techniques, or whether Buchan later slipped the bands over the canoe.

Recent analysis shows that the bark comes from mountain ash, which grows in the ranges east of Melbourne. This suggests that Wurundjeri steered the canoe 50 or more kilometres down the Yarra, moving through their land. The return journey, later in the season, would have been made by foot, the canoe being left to rot slowly by the river. RG

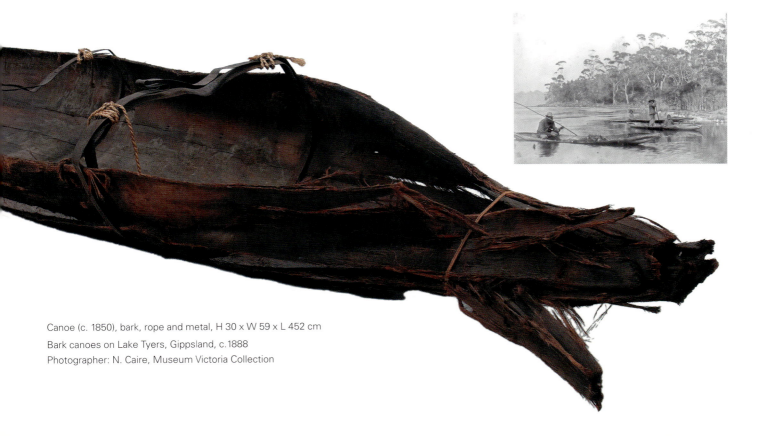

Canoe (c. 1850), bark, rope and metal, H 30 x W 59 x L 452 cm
Bark canoes on Lake Tyers, Gippsland, c.1888
Photographer: N. Caire, Museum Victoria Collection

Fibre apron

Objects made of fragile materials are lucky to survive the rigours of time. This apron from the Wimmera River is one of only six from Aboriginal Victoria in the museum's collection. The other five are made of emu feathers and come mainly from the Melbourne region. This apron is made of natural fibre and coloured with red ochre. Such aprons were usually worn by women. Although an item of everyday use, it is stunning for the beauty of its simple form and rich colouring. This item came to the museum in 1888 from the estate of H.A. Smith. GS

Apron (19th century), hair string, fur string, ochre and sinew,
L 45 x W 14 cm

Tasmanian basket

This Tasmanian Aboriginal basket lay unheralded in the museum's collection for many years after it was acquired from the widow of Archibald Meston in 1954. The basket's maker and history were traced by Gaye Sculthorpe, an Aboriginal Tasmanian who was employed in the museum's anthropology department in the early 1980s. The museum's letter of acquisition noted that the basket had been 'obtained from a quarter-caste living near Oyster Cove' in Tasmania. One of Gaye's elderly relatives told her that she used to have a little basket made by Fanny Cochrane Smith (Gaye's grandmother's grandmother) but that she had given it to the schools' inspector, Mr Meston. Fanny (c. 1834–1905) was not only the creator of the basket but also the only Tasmanian Aboriginal person to record Aboriginal songs and music.

This basket and associated story show the importance of making connections between the museum's objects and those who have cultural and historical links with them. Without such connections, objects remain 'anonymous' and disconnected from their histories. GS

Basket (19th century), woven white flag iris, H 8.5 x diam. 13.5 cm

Indigenous Cultures

Charles Walter photographic album

This is both the oldest photographic album and the oldest group of photographs in the collections of the museum. The images are of residents of Coranderrk Aboriginal Station, Healesville, Victoria.

After seeing one of Charles Walter's images in the *Illustrated Australian News* of August 1865, Sir Redmond Barry commissioned Walter to take photographs for the Intercolonial Exhibition of 1866. This was the first time that photographs of Aboriginal people had been exhibited. Walter's images were catalogued under the title 'Addenda' in the Fine Arts Gallery of the hall. They were subsequently displayed in the 1872 London International Exhibition and the following year in the Vienna Universal Exhibition.

The handwritten notes that make up the caption state: 'Simon Wonga – King of the Yarra Tribe. Son of the former King and King himself for at least 20 years. A great orator in his native language'. Simon Wonga led the first Aboriginal deputation to Melbourne to present the Governor with gifts for the Queen. Wonga died in 1875.

Unlike many of the photographers of the time, Walter refused to reproduce his commissioned images for sale within the tourist market. And again unlike many of his contemporaries, Walter did not seem interested in capturing a 'racial type'; his portraits do not fit easily into the anthropological mode of photography. However, at the same time, little is revealed of the grim circumstances in which the people he was photographing were living.

The original owner of the album was John Green, superintendent of Coranderrk, and it is his annotations we can see today. The album was donated to the museum by his grandson, John Green Parkinson, in 1968. LP

Simon Wonga, albumen print
Charles Walter photo album (1866–67), H 27.9 x W 36.9 cm

Treasures of the Museum

Le Souëf box

The Le Souëf box, a varnished wooden chest decorated with vignettes of pre-contact Aboriginal life in the 1840s, was made by Caroline and Albert Le Souëf in Melbourne in the 1860s. The box contains a set of miniaturised Aboriginal weapons carved by Albert (1828–1902). Caroline (1834–1915), an artist in her own right, made the detailed and delicate ink drawings on the outside of the box, depicting scenes of life of the Taungurong people, indigenous to the Goulburn River region in Victoria. Albert was the son of William Le Souëf, who was dismissed as an Assistant Protector of Aborigines in this region in 1843, while Caroline was the daughter of English squatters who arrived there around the same time. As children, they had close contact with the Taungurong people during a period of aggressive pastoral expansion in south-eastern Australia between the 1830s and 1850s, marked by dispossession of Aboriginal people from their lands. The box reflects the Le Souëfs' childhood experiences, and their lifelong interest in Aboriginal people.

The Le Souëfs created three sets of decorated boxes filled with miniature weapons. This one, exhibited at the 1866 Melbourne Intercolonial Exhibition, goes to the heart of the colonial encounter, for it embodies many of the key concerns of the 19th century's apprehension and representation of Australian Aboriginal people. Ethnography, typology, museology, miniaturisation and a fascination with Indigenous weaponry are just some of the forces at play in this chest, made for instruction and display. The box, intriguing for its assembly of tiny objects, images and annotations, is akin to a mini-museum, and reveals as much about the scholarly concerns of colonial Australia as it does about Aboriginal people. PE

Box and miniature weapons (1860s), ink on wood, box H 15.5 x W 102 x D 15 cm

Indigenous Cultures

Proclamation board

This proclamation board, issued around 1830, represents an attempt by Lieutenant Governor George Arthur of Van Diemen's Land (Tasmania) to conciliate Aboriginal people amid aggressive settlement and frontier violence. Arthur had declared martial law in November 1828 against the 'several Black or Aboriginal natives within the several Districts of the Island'. Three months later, Surveyor General George Frankland, who was also a linguist and artist, suggested to Arthur that 'in the absence of successful communication with these unfortunate people with whose language we are totally unacquainted . . . it might be possible . . . to impart to them . . . the real wishes of the government towards them'. Frankland had seen drawings by Aboriginal people on the bark of trees, and intrigued by this 'newly discovered faculty' he sketched a series of Aboriginal and European figures, showing friendship and equality before the British law. It was, however, to the white man's ways Aboriginal people would adapt.

Frankland recommended that the boards be 'fastened to trees in those remote situations where the natives are most likely to see them'. When, in 1830, the government's intention to produce such pictographs was announced, the *Colonial Times* noted sardonically that the cause of Aboriginal hostility must be 'more deeply probed, or their taste as connoisseurs of paintings be more clearly established'. Soon after, Arthur instigated the operation known as the 'Black Line': an attempt to capture or force Aboriginal people into the Forestier Peninsula. Frankland was at Arthur's side throughout this violent exercise.

This proclamation board comes from the collection of George Augustus Robinson, who Arthur selected to conciliate Aboriginal Tasmanians, and it is believed he carried such boards. Later, he became Chief Protector of the Aborigines in the Port Phillip Bay area, Victoria. PE

Proclamation board (c. 1830), paint on wood, H 33 x W 22.5 cm

Treasures of the Museum

Sedge eel trap and mat

This fibre work is by Joyce Moate, a Taungurong elder. In 1995, the museum purchased the first basket Joyce had made. An eel trap was then commissioned for the opening exhibitions of the Immigration Museum. The trap, like the basket, is an extraordinary piece, with no known equivalent in any museum collection.

Joyce acknowledges the influences of 19th-century baskets made by women at Coranderrk Aboriginal Station, together with photographs taken there: 'That's the first basket I made. It's like the old ones. Dot Peters taught me but I only had three stitches. I learned from the photos too. Then I went to Galeena Beek and looked at the baskets and copied from the old museum ones. I just did the stitch and went from there.'

Joyce also appears to have drawn upon her own memory or understanding of traditional Taungurong forms. She is a grand-daughter of John Patterson, who as a little boy walked with his family and others across the Black Spur in the Dandenong Ranges in 1863 to settle at Coranderrk Aboriginal Station at Badgers Creek near Healesville.

Joyce has continued working with fibres, combining experimentation with indigenous plants and her own creative flair. She now sources all the plant material 'out bush', although originally she grew sedges and grasses in 44-gallon drums in her backyard. Joyce uses mostly sedges and a range of grasses to create patterns by combining materials with varying colour and texture.

Joyce donated this sedge mat to the museum; she described it as 'her own design' as distinct from the 'old ones'. LA

Joyce Moate, eel trap (1996), sedge, L 180 cm
Joyce Moate, mat (1997), sedge and tussock grass, diam. 142 cm

Indigenous Cultures

Wurreka

Wurreka is the curved, etched zinc wall in Bunjilaka, the museum's Aboriginal centre. It was commissioned as part of the building works of the new museum after a competition to select a design. Judy Watson, a Waanyi artist from Queensland, was the winner.

Judy worked with local Aboriginal communities and artists in developing the design. She spent four months in Melbourne in 1999, travelling around Victoria, talking to people, visiting cultural sites and looking at objects. Aboriginal community members visited the project at the Australian Print Workshop, where the panels were etched, and suggested symbols and objects for inclusion. The work developed in an organic fashion over several months – a process Judy called 'an ongoing conversation' – and 74 panels of etched designs were produced. The images etched in the wall reflect the unique environment of south-eastern Australia and objects from this region housed in the museum's collections, such as eel traps, baskets, clubs and necklaces.

'*Wurreka*' means 'to speak' in the Wemba Wemba language of north-western Victoria. In Judy's words: 'I hope that *Wurreka* will be a "learning wall" and a resource for people, particularly children, wanting to learn about Victoria's Aboriginal culture. I want the work to have a fluid, dreamlike quality, objects will be floating across the panels, as though on the edge of memory. It is about survival, resilience, resistance and strength'. GS

Judy Watson, *Wurreka* details (1999), etched zinc, H 240 x W 3500 cm

Treasures of the Museum

Lionel Rose's boxing gown

Lionel Rose wore this gown on the night he defeated Fighting Harada in Tokyo on 26 February 1968 to become world bantamweight boxing champion. That fight made Lionel Rose a national hero overnight. When he returned to Melbourne he was greeted by a crowd of 250 000 people; 10 times the number the Beatles had attracted four years earlier. This fight was a key event in Rose's sporting history and in the history of Indigenous boxing. Through this and subsequent fights, Rose became a household name in Australia and an Australian sporting hero. He was awarded an MBE and was Australian of the Year in 1968, finally retiring in 1975 at the age of 27.

Lionel Rose is a Gunditjmara man. He grew up at Jacksons Track, near Drouin in Victoria. His rise to international fame from the most impoverished circumstances has made him an inspiration to Aboriginal people, and today he remains one of Australia's greatest Indigenous sports heroes. GF

Boxing gown, satin, L 117 x W 99 cm

Indigenous Cultures

Rainforest shield

In the 1870s and 1880s, many painted shields and bicornial baskets were collected in north-eastern Queensland. The shields were made from the buttress roots of large rainforest trees and were of great interest to private collectors and scientists who visited this new northern frontier. Walter Roth, an Aboriginal Protector in northern Queensland, noted '. . . little bartering continued between Aboriginal groups of the region'. The shields had been part of a 'southern foreign trade' from the Mulgrave River. Young men had to demonstrate their ability to handle these shields, as well as a large wooden sword. At the end of the initiation they were given a blank shield on which were painted totemic designs such as this scorpion.   LA

Rainforest blanket

In the late 1800s, a thriving trade in artefacts occurred in Atherton, Babinda, Cardwell, Herbert River, Kuranda, Russell River and the Tully River in northern Queensland. These were depots for the distribution of rations and blankets to Aboriginal people, and they became well known to private collectors and photographers. Walter Roth recorded the making of bark blankets from the inner bark of a fig tree at Atherton around 1900. Thin sheets of bark were peeled off and made pliable using a wooden beater. The bark blanket was then folded into a small bundle to carry inside a dilly bag. This extremely rare painted example was collected on the Tully River around 1928.   LA

Shield (c. 1890s), natural pigments on wood, H 96 x W 37 cm

Blanket (c. 1928), natural pigment on bark, H 79 x W 114 cm

Treasures of the Museum

Decorated container

Erlikilyika (c. 1865–c. 1930), also known as Jim Kite, was a southern Arrernte man who was a gifted carver, tracker, linguist and interpreter. He accompanied Walter Baldwin Spencer, director of the National Museum of Victoria, and Frank Gillen on their journey 'across Australia' in 1901–02. Erlikilyika received acclaim in Alice Springs for the fine sculpted figures he made from china clay using a pocketknife and wires. Clay smoking pipes with images of local identities, dingoes, horses, eagle claws, hands and eggs carved into the bowls were popular. The surfaces of wooden artefacts by Erlikilyika featured scenes of Aboriginal life, insects and historical events, such as the overland journey of explorer John McDouall Stuart in the 1840s. LA

Rainforest basket

Bicornial baskets, made of split lawyer vine, come from the rainforest and adjacent coastal areas of north-eastern Queensland around Cairns. Both men and women made these baskets, and carried food and personal belongings in them. The two-cornered base made the basket ideal to use as a trap and sieve when secured in a stream. They were traded from Cardwell north to Port Douglas and exchanged for bark blankets with people from the Tully River area. Anthropologist Ursula McConnell recorded an important story place at Mission Bay that includes a representation of a 'lawyer cane dilly bag'. LA

Detail of a container attributed to Erlikilyika, natural pigments on carved wood, H 6 x W 48 x D 12.5 cm

Bicornial basket (c. 1890s), split lawyer vine, H 59.5 x W 56 x D 38 cm

Indigenous Cultures

Pandanus bags

The creation of fibre work has a long history in northern Australia. Images of dilly bags appear in the oldest sequence of rock paintings in western Arnhem Land, dating from around 20 000 years ago. Ancestors gave Aboriginal people fibre work, sacred versions of which are painted or else decorated with feathers for ceremony. These bags from western Arnhem Land are 90 years old. They are made of fibre produced from the dried and split leaves of the pandanus palm. Women across Arnhem Land continue to produce these bags, which are important cultural forms, enshrined in traditions of great artistry and detailed technical knowledge. LA

Sedge grass bags

Sedge grass dilly bags are made using a conventional twined form from Arnhem Land, in which two strands are interlaced with a weft element. The material and technique is also used for mats, sieves and traps. These are commonly referred to as hunting bags because of their strength. They are not coloured or decorated. Vegetable foods, meat and fish are carried in larger dilly bags, and small ones are used as sieves. The bags here span a 50-year period, with the oldest one being collected by anthropologist Donald Thomson in 1936 and the others from Maningrida being made in the late 1980s. LA

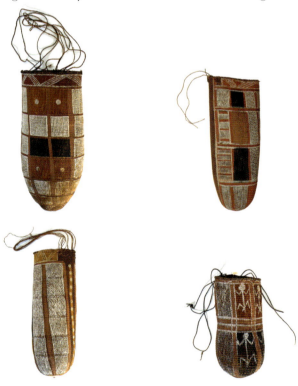

1–2

3–4

Bags (c. 1912–13), natural pigments on pandanus leaf,
H 43–76 × diam. 14–24 cm

1 Hunting bag (c. 1936), sedge, H 113.5 × W 51 × D 28 cm
Donald Thomson Collection, on loan from the University of Melbourne
2–4 Hunting bags (c. 1989), sedge, H 60–69 × diam. 24.5–29 cm

Treasures of the Museum

Mimih figures

The museum has an impressive array of figurative carvings from Arnhem Land, including the mischievous spirits called *mimihs*. These live in caves and rock shelters in the stone country of western Arnhem Land, where they left their shadows behind in rock art that is a few thousand years old. They are long, slender figures often depicted either in flight chasing kangaroos or dancing. Two of these figures, the second and fourth from the left, were made at Barrihdjowkkeng, an outstation near Maningrida and home of the most famous carver of *mimihs*, the late Kunwinjku artist Crusoe Kuningbal. LA

Mimih figures (1972, n.d., 1978, n.d.), natural pigments on wood, H 15.5–193 x diam. 7–15.5 cm
Christensen Collection

Treasures of the Museum

Tunga

Purukuparli and Bima were among the first Tiwi people, and Purukuparli passed down the correct way to bury the dead – the dances, the songs and the designs. A ceremony is held at the graveside about six months after burial, and relatives paint their bodies with designs to hide their identity from *mapurtiti*, the harmful spirits of the dead. Painted bark containers called *tunga* are broken over the carved and painted poles erected in a circle around the grave. Walter Baldwin Spencer collected an extraordinary array of these containers, each painted with a unique design, from Bathurst and Melville islands between 1911 and 1915. LA

Tiwi carving

The Tiwi people of Bathurst and Melville islands are well known for elaborate carved and painted grave posts, called *tutini*, erected during ceremonies marking the end of the mourning period, or *pukamani*. Human figures appeared on these grave posts as early as the 1920s, but the practice of carving freestanding forms emerged during the 1970s as markets for small carvings increased. By the late 1970s, Ketiminawlunggawi, also known as Declan Apuatimi (c. 1930–85), was the most famous Tiwi artist and known particularly for his figurative ironwood carvings. The growing market meant that artists such Declan were able to consolidate their careers. LA

Tunga (c. 1912), natural pigments on bark, H 45 x W 42 cm

Carved figure (c. 1979) attributed to Declan Apuatimi, natural pigments on ironwood, H 33 x diam. 17 cm
Christensen Collection

Indigenous Cultures

Haasts Bluff

Albert Namatjira (1902–59) painted *Haasts Bluff* for the first exhibition of watercolours from Hermannsburg Mission in 1938. After the first three days of the exhibition at the Lower Town Hall in Melbourne, all 41 works had sold. This marked the beginning of Namatjira's successful career as an artist; by the 1940s he was a household name. He was the first Aboriginal person to be granted Australian citizenship, in 1957, but he was denied the same fundamental rights and freedoms his white contemporaries took for granted.

Namatjira's artistic talent lives on through western Arrernte watercolour painting. He encouraged and taught others to paint in watercolours, and particular styles have emerged within specific families or groups of painters. Since the 1950s, women have also painted in watercolours. Acclaimed artist Clifford Possum Tjapaltjarri learned watercolour techniques from one of Namatjira's sons at Papunya. Namatjira had lived at times at Papunya with his wife, Ilkalita, a Luritja woman who had family there. When Luritja people came in from the desert in the 1930s they also settled at Haasts Bluff, which is depicted in this work. Other Aboriginal artists, such as Bluey Roberts, the late Ginger Riley and the late Lin Onus, also spoke of Namatjira's influence on them.

In the past, Namatjira's work was excluded from many of Australia's major museums and art galleries. His watercolours were considered to be outside Aboriginal tradition, but it is now understood that the landscapes he painted reflect close connections to western Arrernte country and specific totemic sites. The museum holds a number of excellent contemporary and historical watercolours by western Arrernte artists. LA

Albert Namatjira, *Haasts Bluff* (1938), watercolour on wove paper, H 61 x W 48.5 cm

Treasures of the Museum

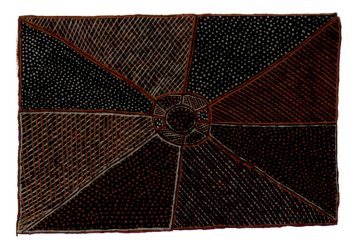

Jilamara

Fifteen artworks were completed by Tiwi artists in 1992 when James Bennett, then the art advisor at Jilamara Arts and Crafts at Milikapiti on Melville Island, organised 11 artists to paint with ochres on paper for the first time. The museum purchased this collection of works that depict *jilamara* or 'old designs'.

The group included well-known senior Tiwi women, including the wife of the famous Tiwi carver and painter Declan Apuatimi. Jean Baptist Apuatimi (1930–) was taught to paint by her husband, who she recalls saying, 'One day you will be an artist – you will take my place'. LA

Murayana bark painting

Murayana is the major ancestor for the Daygurrgurr Gupapuyngu people of north-eastern Arnhem Land. Their ancestral home is Djiliwirri on the western coast of Buckingham Bay near Howard Island. Murayana travels from Djiliwirri on his journey north-east, and on his body can be seen the distinctive Gupapuyngu honey clan pattern.

Joseph Neparrnga Gumbula is a Daygurrgurr Gupapuyngu elder and a son of the artist Djawa Dhäwirringu (c. 1905–85). On selecting this work to be included in the book, Neparrnga explained, 'We don't do visual art. We paint our country and ancestors . . . The paintings were taken into the garma [public domain] [when Djawa] painted on barks for selling'. LA

Jean Baptist Apuatimi, *Jilamara* (1992), natural pigments on lanaquarelle paper, H 57.5 x W 76.7 cm

Djawa Dhäwirringu, untitled (c. 1960), natural pigments on bark, H 35.5 x W 65 cm

Indigenous Cultures

Ngalyod Devours a Hunter

Ngalyod, the rainbow serpent, is one of the most important ancestor spirits of western Arnhem Land and lives in the area south and east of Gunbalanya (formerly Oenpelli). Images of Ngalyod appear in rock paintings of the region and are over 20 000 years old. Ngalyod is much feared and can destroy anyone who breaks the law. Children who wander away from camp are likely to be taken by the serpent's spirit, which lives in waterholes and rock shelters.

Ngalyod takes a variety of forms, and only Kuninjku men of senior ceremonial status can paint this image. While stylistic variations of Ngalyod occur, rules are adhered to in painting this and other images. Artists may paint only the ancestors to which they have inherited rights through their father. Ancestors such as Ngalyod must be painted 'accurately' and exhibit a range of figurative elements. For example, the rainbow serpent can be painted with some features of a kangaroo, such as the ears or head. The use of crosshatching, or *rarrk*, indicates the sacred, ceremonial associations of the ancestor, and colours must be applied in the correct order.

Ngalyod Devours a Hunter was painted by Njiminjuma (1945–) at Mumeka outstation in December 1979. It typifies the style of bark painters from Mumeka, who use the intricate crosshatching patterning to infill the entire body of the ancestor. This painting depicts the story of a hunter who speared a kangaroo that was in fact the rainbow serpent. Changing back into its original form, Ngalyod devours the hunter. LA

Njiminjuma, *Ngalyod Devours a Hunter* (1979), natural pigments on bark, H 116 x W 64 cm
Licensed by Viscopy, 2004

Treasures of the Museum

Gagadju bark painting

The museum's collection of over 500 Arnhem Land bark paintings began with 38 works from the Alligator River area of western Arnhem Land, collected in 1912 by Walter Baldwin Spencer. The paintings were removed from bark living shelters built for protection from wet season rains.

This painting depicts the ancestor identified by Spencer as 'Yungwalia, who lives in caves among the hills'. The ancestor is carrying a bunch of feathers used during dances, and a club is in his right hand 'in case he should have to fight a hostile Yungwalia belonging to another country'. LA

1

Mildjingi bark painting

This magnificent painting was collected in central Arnhem Land by anthropologist Donald Thomson in 1937. It depicts ceremonial designs painted on the torsos of young men during the final stages of a sacred *Ngarra* ceremony. The images are saltwater fish that relate to the travels of two ancestors that took the form of dogs. The story is so important that the dogs themselves are never depicted nor discussed openly.

This is an open or public version of the sacred dog story. During their travels, one of the dogs walked into the sea, stood up and spat salt water into the air. Clouds formed from the vapour and brought on the wet season rains, represented by small white dots. As clouds built up, the ancestral mackerel came in from the sea and the stingray came into the shallow water. Thomson recorded the fish on the bottom as *dhinimbu*, the name for mackerel or tuna. Their appearance, chasing schools of little fish, is a seasonal indicator. Their 'flash in the water' means the wind is due from the north-east and monsoon clouds will follow. LA

2

1 Artist unknown, untitled (c. 1912), natural pigments on bark, H 37.5 x W 126 cm
2 Artist unknown, untitled (1937), natural pigments on bark, H 126 x W 61.5 cm
Donald Thomson Collection, on loan from the University of Melbourne

Indigenous Cultures

Tjapu bark painting

Over 60 years ago, with the advice, support and cooperation of key clan leaders from across eastern Arnhem Land, Donald Thomson hand-picked a group of around 50 Yolngu men that included 'many renowned warriors'. They formed the nucleus of the Northern Territory Special Reconnaissance Unit, whose objective was to defend 1600 kilometres of Australia's northern coastline against Japanese attack. A permanent base camp was established in August 1942 at Caledon Bay, where representatives of each clan remained with key leaders. Nine paintings were completed over two days at that camp in September. The paintings relate to the inland and saltwater clan estates of the Dhalwangu, Madarrpa, Ritharrngu and Tjapu clans of north-eastern Arnhem Land.

This painting by Wonggu (c. 1884–1958), the famous Tjapu clan leader and warrior, depicts a prau and the activities of Macassan fishermen who came to the northern coastline annually to collect trepang, or bêche-de-mer. Vertical bands on either side of the painting indicate a day's activities of fishermen collecting and preparing trepang. The white crosshatched section on the right indicates that it is early in the day, and the band infilled with black on the left shows it is sunset. The canoe, or *lippa lippa*, in the upper right shows a man diving onto the reef for trepang; others hunt turtle for its much-prized shell. In the lower left, three groups of men (some wearing trousers and belts) are boiling trepang in large cooking pots before drying it.

Wonggu inherited the rights to paint these designs through his maternal grandmother, or *mari*. They relate to an important saltwater place in the sea off Yarrinya in Munyuku clan country in the north-western corner of Blue Mud Bay. LA

Wonggu Mununggurr, untitled (1942), natural pigments on bark,
H 18.2 × W 80 cm
Donald Thomson Collection, on loan from the University of Melbourne

Indigenous Cultures

The Dawn of Art (c. 1888), lead and coloured pencil on paper, H 81.5 x W 166.5 cm

The Dawn of Art

These drawings were one set in a series that formed the first exhibition of Aboriginal art, entitled *The Dawn of Art*. John George Knight, as deputy sheriff of Palmerston (now Darwin), was commissioned to prepare the Northern Territory courts for the 1888 Centennial International Exhibition in the Exhibition Building in Melbourne. The pencil drawings were exhibited in framed sets, and this is the only complete set that has survived in its original frame.

Knight was responsible for the welfare and reform of prison inmates in Darwin's Fannie Bay Jail. He recognised the artistic talents of the Aboriginal prisoners and collected works by them for the Melbourne exhibition. Jemmy Miller (Ilon-tereba; c. 1851–unknown), who was serving a sentence of life imprisonment, was a Wulwulan man from the Pine Creek and South Alligator River area of the Northern Territory, but little is known of the Aboriginal prisoner Paddy (Min-dil-pil-dil), who produced most of the drawings for Knight. The police and courts in Palmerston retained Billiamook (Gapal, or Billy Muck; c.1853–unknown), a Larrakia man, as an interpreter.

These works remained unknown and unregistered in the collection for more than 70 years, until the frame was located during the final stages of the museum's relocation to Carlton Gardens in September 2001. The University of Melbourne's Department of Zoology had sent the drawings to the museum in 1929; however, it is not known when the university obtained them. Eighteen drawings from the *Dawn of Art* were transferred from the South Australian School of Art to the South Australian Museum in 1958. LA

Top row from left: Paddy (Min-dil-pil-dil), untitled; Billiamook (Gapal), untitled; Paddy (Min-dil-pil-dil), untitled
Bottom row from left: Billiamook (Gapal), untitled; Paddy (Min-dil-pil-dil), untitled; Jemmy Miller (Ilon-tereba), untitled

Jandamarra's boomerang

Jandamarra's boomerang is striking in its simplicity. This beautifully balanced, fluted boomerang from the west Kimberleys, Western Australia, is distinguished by three large oval markings – one at the apex and one on each wing. One side bears an old label: 'Western Australian Boomerang called Kielie of curious pattern. This boomerang belonged to the black bushranger Pidgeon who was shot by the police on . . . the Lillemillora Gorge, Leopold Range. Rare Pattern'.

Pidgeon, now known by his Aboriginal name 'Jandamarra', was the leader of the Bunuba resistance in the Napier Range during the mid-1890s, and is a character of mythic proportions. His status, and in many ways his short life, parallels that of the Irish–Australian hero Ned Kelly.

Accused and jailed for stealing stock, Jandamarra missed the education necessary to become a man in traditional Bunuba society. Instead, he attracted the attention of successive European mentors, becoming a skilled horseman, fist fighter and marksman of unequalled accuracy. Inevitably, he was recruited as a police tracker. Constable Bill Richardson engaged Jandamarra to join him on a foray into Bunuba country in 1894, where they captured 17 prisoners, including Elemarra, a legendary leader of Bunuba resistance to the pastoralists.

In the dead of night on 31 October, Jandamarra shot Richardson, releasing his countrymen and fleeing to the safety of the limestone parapets of the Napier Range.

A week later, Jandamarra and his followers ambushed advancing cattle drovers at Windjana Pool, but two stock boys escaped to tell the tale. The Kimberley pastoralists and Perth's political establishment were in uproar, commissioning a succession of punitive raids on the Bunuba; oral history tells that scores of people were massacred.

Indigenous Cultures

It was not until Micki, an Aboriginal man from the Pilbara, was recruited that the revenge party got close to Jandamarra. The fatal confrontation occurred at Tunnel Creek, where Micki fired his rifle and Jandamarra plummeted 30 metres to his death.

While the exact provenance of the boomerang is unknown, it is likely to have been abandoned by Jandamarra after a battle at the Two Mile Creek homestead, where police found guns, ammunition and native weapons. The boomerang was donated to the museum by geologist E. J. Dunn.

If Jandamarra's boomerang were taken from the museum store and thrown into the sky, it would spin on the white oval at its centre, its outer ovals merging to form a second circle. The resulting target-like motif was prophetic for the hero who was wanted 'dead or alive' by the pastoralists wishing to occupy Bunuba land. JK

Boomerang (late 19th century), natural pigments on wood,
L 52.5 x W 7.4 cm, weight 248 gm

Treasures of the Museum

Massacre and Rover Thomas Story – Texas Downs Country

This painting records two incidents that occurred on Texas Downs Station in the Kimberleys in Western Australia. The events are divided by the line that represents Horseshoe Creek. The upper scene depicts a massacre that took place early in the 20th century. It is part of Aboriginal oral history but is not reflected in Western written histories of the area. The images represent a time when Aboriginal men killed a bullock on the station. They were pursued and shot by white men (represented by the white hats) and the bodies were then burned in an attempt to disguise the incident.

The scene depicted in the lower half of the painting represents an incident when Rover Thomas and his wife, Queenie (c. 1930–98), were out mustering and Rover was thrown from his horse. The horse trod on his head and scalped him. Queenie boiled a needle and sewed his scalp back on, saving Rover's life. In later years, Queenie and Rover Thomas became two of the most significant Aboriginal artists from the Kimberley region, with strong national and international reputations. In 1998, Queenie was declared a State Living Treasure for her commitment to the arts and to teaching the Kija language.

This painting is both a monument to memory and a wonderful depiction of country. It offers interpretations of the past that are not part of the official records. It is also a distinctive landscape painting and is representative of work from the Kimberleys region, with the use of white dots to define major features of the landscape. Part of the Spirit Country Collection, the painting was donated by the Gantner Myer family to the museum in 2002. This collection was formed over a four-year period by Australian art patrons and philanthropists Carrillo Gantner and Baillieu Myer, with assistance from Neilma Gantner and curator Jennifer Isaacs. LP

Queenie McKenzie, *Massacre and Rover Thomas Story – Texas Downs Country* (1996), ochre and clay on canvas, H 140 x W 100 cm
Gantner Myer Collection
Courtesy of Red Rock Art

Indigenous Cultures

Kimberley glass points

Aboriginal stone tools can be found throughout Australia, yet few match the level of craftsmanship exhibited in the small cutting blades known as Kimberley points. As the name implies, they originate in the Kimberley region of north-western Australia. Although the points were originally made of stone, the use of glass and various ceramic materials became widespread following contact with Europeans in the late 19th century. A sophisticated pressure-flaking technique was developed to produce a sharp cutting edge on the glass points; this also gave them their unique beauty. The points are still manufactured in a few remote communities in the Kimberleys by a dwindling number of Aboriginal craftsmen. PB

Kimberley points (late 19th century), glass, stone and ceramic,
L 8 x W 2.5 cm (average)

Treasures of the Museum

Pintupi spearthrower

Spearthrowers were commonly used by Aboriginal people in Central Australia. This example has special historical significance as it was collected by anthropologist Donald Thomson during an expedition to a remote corner of Central Australia in 1957. Thomson wished to locate the Pintupi people, an Aboriginal group who had experienced little if any contact with Europeans. This spearthrower was given to Thomson by one of the Pintupi men he encountered during the trip. Carved into the spearthrower is a series of concentric circles and lines depicting significant waterholes, creeks and claypans in Pintupi country. PB

Stone axes and picks

These stone axes and picks were made by the Warumungu and Tjingali groups from Tenant Creek in Central Australia. The blades of the picks are made from quartzite using techniques similar to those employed in the making of stone knives, as shown on the facing page. The axe heads are produced from diorite and usually take several days to make. A suitable stone block is found and carefully chipped into a shape. It is then smoothed down on a flat quartzite stone, using water and sand as a grinding medium. Once all traces of the chipping have been removed, a split wooden handle is attached, using spinifex resin and vegetable fibre string. PB

Spearthrower (1957), mulga wood, L 77 x W 12 cm
Donald Thomson Collection, on loan from the University of Melbourne

Axes (early 20th century), diorite, spinifex resin, mulga wood and vegetable fibre, axes L 50 x W 20 cm (average), picks L 40 x W 25 cm (average)

Indigenous Cultures

Decorated knives and sheaths

These rare Aboriginal stone knives were collected by Walter Baldwin Spencer and Frank Gillen during an expedition to Central Australia in 1901–02. The knives were manufactured by people from the Warumungu and Tjingali groups near Tenant Creek. The blades are made from quartzite stone, which is still available at several quarries in the region. The handles are fashioned from carved lengths of mulga wood and spinifex resin. Some knives had a sheath manufactured from strips of bark from the paperbark tree and other sheaths were made from feathers. The decorations on the handles are composed of natural pigments, including charcoal, yellow ochre and white pipe clay. Although Spencer and Gillen did not record the meaning of these designs, they appear to represent – in iconographic form – the various totemic ancestors associated with either the maker or owner of the knives. Of particular interest is the close resemblance these designs have with contemporary forms of Aboriginal art from Central Australia.

Although unsuitable for cutting wood, the knives were indispensable for butchering kangaroo, emu, possum and other game. They were also used for a number of customary purposes, including ritualised fighting, initiation and other ceremonies. For example, during mourning rituals, men who stood in a certain relationship with a dead relative were obliged to cut their thighs and shoulders with these knives as a mark of respect for the deceased. PB

Knives and sheaths (1901–02), quartzite, spinifex resin, charcoal, yellow ochre, white pipe clay, paper bark, hair string and feathers, L 20 x W 4 cm (average)

Treasures of the Museum

Pearl-shell ornaments

Pearl shells like the ones depicted here were used in rain-making ceremonies by Aboriginal groups across Central Australia. The zigzag-shaped lines carved into some of the shells represent sheets of lightning associated with storm clouds, and the dots between the lines are droplets of rain. The anthropologist C.P. Mountford recorded a ritual ceremony conducted by the Pitjantjatjara people in which similar shells were used in a successful attempt to produce rain. The shells generally originated in Broome, Western Australia, and were highly prized objects of trade. Some examples have been found as far afield as Port Augusta in South Australia. PB

Pearl-shell ornaments (20th century), incised and decorated with red ochre and charcoal, approx. L 18 x W 15 cm

Indigenous Cultures

Body ornaments

The Aboriginal people of Central Australia produced a variety of body ornaments for both ceremonial and decorative purposes. Headbands, armlets, aprons, pubic tassels, pendants, neckbands and other ornaments were made from materials such as human-hair string, feathers, animal bones and spinifex resin. Figure 2 is composed of kangaroo teeth embedded in a resin pendant with a hair-string cord. This item was generally worn by women as a headband with the pendant placed over the forehead. In some cases, these ornaments were 'sung' to give them certain magical powers and were traded between neighbouring groups. PB

2–5

1 Forehead ornament (1916), kangaroo teeth in beeswax, L 45 x W 9.5 cm
2 Forehead ornament (1902), kangaroo teeth in spinifex resin, L 17 x W 5.5 cm
3 Neck band (1899), hair string, Eagle-hawk claws and resin, L 43 x W 4 cm
4 Neck ornament (1907), hair string and small marsupial mandible, L 50 x W 3 cm
5 Headband (1902), fur string and kangaroo teeth, L 42 x W 9 cm

Treasures of the Museum

Mourning headdress

It was once customary for an Arrernte woman of Central Australia to wear a special headdress following the death of her husband. The headdress, or *chimurillia*, was meant to show the spirit of the dead husband that the man had been mourned in a correct manner. If a widow failed to wear the headdress, it was believed that the spirit of the husband would return and cause sickness and misfortune among the living. This example was acquired by Walter Baldwin Spencer near Alice Springs in 1901 and is the only surviving object of its type. PB

Arrernte woman wearing a mourning headdress, 1901
Photographer: Walter Balwin Spencer, Museum Victoria Collection

Headdress (1899), animal bones, spinifex resin and hair string,
L 48.5 x W 40.5 cm

Indigenous Cultures

1–2

3

Ceremonial headdresses

Elaborate headdresses and other ceremonial ornaments were often used in rituals performed by Aboriginal people. These headdresses were collected by ethnographer George Horne in 1921 from Mungerainie Bore, a small settlement east of Lake Eyre North, in South Australia. This remote area is home to the Wangkanguru people who made these headdresses, or *charpoo*. According to Horne, the headdresses were used in a welcoming ceremony known as the *mindiri*, performed by a large group of men near Mungerainie. As was customary, whenever one group of men travelled to another's country, their visit had to be sanctioned through a special ceremony conducted by both the hosts and visitors. In this way, any outstanding conflicts that existed between the groups could be absolved ritually while the visitors remained on foreign soil. Moreover, the welcoming ceremony gave the visitors the authority to use local water and food supplies during their stay. Such ceremonies often involved the re-telling of dreaming stories through the use of body decorations and dance movements. The welcoming ceremony in which these headdresses were used concerned an emu ancestor, *muramura warugati*, and described his travels across Wangkanguru country. By wearing the headdresses and performing the ceremony, the Wangkanguru men could not only demonstrate that they were the ritual owners of the emu story, but the owners of the land from which the story emanated. Thus, the visitors would be obliged to accept the authority of the Wangkanguru men in welcoming them into their country. PB

1 Headdress (1897), rabbit tail tips, kangaroo and hair string, L 41 x W 24.5 cm

2 Headdress (1922), rabbit tails and hair string, L 70 x W 56 cm

3 Headdress (1924), rabbit tails and hair string, L 56 x W 34 cm

Treasures of the Museum

Pintupi Men Drinking from a Desert Lake

This photograph was taken by anthropologist Donald Thomson during his expedition to Central Australia in 1957. It depicts a group of Pintupi men drinking from a large pool of water near Lake Mackay in the Northern Territory.

The Pintupi were one of the last Aboriginal groups to encounter Europeans. The most recent 'first contact' occurred in 1984 when a Pintupi family emerged from their desert home near Winparrku, in Western Australia. For the Pintupi, these first encounters were both bewildering and intriguing. For instance, during the 1930s a government survey team flew to a remote location on the eastern edge of Pintupi country, landing close to a Pintupi camp. Having never seen white people before, the Pintupi ran and hid in a clump of mulga trees some distance away. Thinking that the plane might be a *tjulpu mamu* (devil bird), one of the older men tried to kill it using a pointing bone, or *yiri tarrka*. To their amazement, instead of the plane being killed, a *nyikanyika* (man with white skin) emerged from its side. When the plane eventually departed, the Pintupi found pieces of clothing and tins of meat, evidently left by the pilot. Thinking that these items might be harmful, they buried them and hurriedly left the area.

When Thomson took this photograph in 1957, many Pintupi had grown familiar with European intrusions into their country, and at about this time a large group left their lands and walked 600 kilometres into a government ration depot, Haasts Bluff. PB

Pintupi Men Drinking from a Desert Lake (1957)
Photographer: D.F. Thomson, courtesy of Mrs D.M. Thomson

Indigenous Cultures

Pintupi Man with Lizard, Shield and Spear

Lizards once provided the main source of edible meat for the desert-dwelling Pintupi of Central Australia. In this photograph, taken by Donald Thomson in 1957, a Pintupi man displays a freshly caught Perentie Lizard, or *ngintaka*. Apart from lizards and other reptiles, the Pintupi relied on mammals and large birds as a source of protein. These included kangaroos, or *marlu*, emus, or *tjakipirri*, and bush turkeys, or *kipara*. Although such animals were highly prized by the Pintupi, they were not particularly abundant.

Indeed, it has been estimated that up to 80 per cent of the Pintupi diet was based on vegetable foods. A wide variety of edible berries, roots, seeds and flowers can be found throughout the Central Australian desert (many specimens of which were collected by Thomson and deposited in the museum's collection).

To a large extent, the availability of food determined the movement of the Pintupi across their country. Once food resources in a given area were exhausted – which occurred relatively quickly – a family group would move onto a new region. During periods of drought, this nomadic pattern was accentuated due to the need to travel further afield to find food and water. An anthropologist who worked closely with the Pintupi, Fred Myers, has suggested that a Pintupi family would travel within an area of nearly 5000 square kilometres over a year. PB

Pintupi Man with Lizard, Shield and Spear (1957)
Photographer: D.F. Thomson, courtesy of Mrs D.M. Thomson

Treasures of the Museum

Atininga Avenging Party

In general, the Aboriginal people of Central Australia believed that the death of any person was due to the evil influences of another. All deaths therefore had to be avenged. Elaborate rituals were used to establish the identity and location of a murderer, and special procedures were employed to kill them. This photograph depicts an avenging party, or *atininga*, returning to camp after successfully finding and eliminating a man from a neighbouring group accused of murder. The decorations of eucalyptus leaves – placed against the forehead, through the nose and on the shoulders – indicate that the *atininga* men have accomplished their mission. PB

Arrernte Women Holding Sacred Arachitta Poles

The passage from boyhood to manhood was perhaps the most important occasion in the life of an Arrernte man. A series of elaborate initiation ceremonies, extending over a period of months, was performed to enact this transformation. The initiate, or *wurtja*, would not only become a man but would also be given access to the secret ritual life of men. Although the greater part of such ceremonies was strictly forbidden to women, there was a brief moment in the first of these rituals, the *lartna*, where women who had a certain relationship to the initiate would participate. This photograph depicts such a women holding sacred *arachitta* poles, erected on the initiation ground. PB

Atininga Avenging Party Returning to Camp with Decorations Denoting Success (1901)
Photographer: Walter Baldwin Spencer, Museum Victoria Collection

Arrernte Women Holding Sacred Arachitta Poles (1895)
Photographer: Walter Baldwin Spencer, Museum Victoria Collection

Indigenous Cultures

Shell-inlay objects

The frigate birds and bonito fish outlined in inlaid shell are icons representing the importance of the annual visit made by schools of bonito. The first bonito is considered sacred, and its arrival signals the time for ceremonial knowledge of this important fish to be imparted to young initiates on their way to adulthood. Imagine the spectacle of a feeding frenzy where smaller fish are forced by the bonito to the surface where they are also food for diving frigate birds. Sharks add to the melee, and to the danger. Fast canoes and well-prepared and maintained hooks and lines are included in the specialised fishing technology of the Solomon Islands, allowing islanders to take immediate advantage of the bonito's sudden arrival. RV

Carved tuna (early 20th century), wood and pearl shell, H 70 x 115 cm
Bowl (early 20th century), wood and pearl shell, H 32.5 x L 81 cm
Frigate-bird bowl (early 20th century), wood and pearl shell, H 19.5 x L 54 cm

Solomon Islands canoe

Early European visitors to the Solomon Islands remarked on the beauty and grace of the canoes found there. They were constructed from hand-hewn planks attached to each other by cane ties, the whole framework then being mounted and lashed onto ornate internal spreaders, or ribs. The gaps between the planks were plugged with natural putty from the tita nut (*Parinarium laurinum*). Both prow and stern carried designs of inlaid shell, and no two canoes were decorated in the same way.

Large, ocean-going canoes, or *tomako*, in the western Solomons had high prow and stern posts, each of which was surmounted by a pair of figures. Those on the prow looked fore and aft, while those on the stern looked to port and starboard. The spirits looking after the welfare of the canoe and its crew could see in all directions. Perhaps the most remarkable figure was the *nguzunguzu*, a carved head with protruding jaws, painted black and decorated with inlaid nautilus shell. It was mounted

Canoe (19th century), wood and shell, H 52.5 x W 110 x L 1380 cm

Thomas McMahon, *Solomon Islands war canoe*, published in J.A. Hammerton (ed.), *Peoples of All Nations* (1920–38)

Nguzunguzu (c. 1900), wood and shells, H 24.5 x W 12 X D 15.5 cm

Indigenous Cultures

near the waterline on the prow so that it dipped in and out of the water, on the lookout for hostile water spirits.

The vessel on the facing page was a head-hunting canoe from Roviana Lagoon, New Georgia. Santa Isabel, immediately to the north, was a favourite destination for raiding. It was on a trip there in the search for heads in 1901 that the museum's canoe was seized by the colonial administrators. At 14 metres long, the canoe would have held about 18 warriors. RV

Treasures of the Museum

Body armour and spear

The Gilbert Islands (in the Republic of Kiribati) are densely populated, and the islanders depend for their livelihood primarily on coconuts, pandanus and the products of the sea. Disagreements among so many people were once common, and often settled by armed combat between two warriors. Young boys, from an early age, were instructed in the arts of war, in particular how to handle swords and knives, the edges of which were lined with sharks' teeth. Special clothing, made from coconut fibre and woven into a suit of armour, protected the combatants. The dried skin of a Puffer Fish made an adequate helmet to protect the head during combat, while dried shark and ray skin provided protection for other exposed parts of the body. RV

1 Helmet (c. 1850), Puffer Fish, H 34 x diam. 27 cm

2 Under tunic (c. 1850), coconut fibre, L 54 x W 160 cm

3 Chest armour (c. 1850), coconut fibre, L 107 x W 52 cm

4 Leggings (c. 1850), coconut fibre, L 186 x W 44 cm

5 Spear (c. 1850), wood and sharks' teeth L 117 x W 39 cm

6 Kiribati warrior in traditional armour
Photographer: F. H. Duffy, courtesy of Rod Ewins

Indigenous Cultures

Wooden club

The Rarotongan club, made from highly polished ironwood, or toa, must be one of the most beautifully executed in any of the Pacific islands. The clubs are made by skilled, male woodcarvers; the blade is superbly scalloped and the handle decorated near the blade with a single transverse band. Though not an element of this club's design, the handle is often phallic-shaped, thought to accentuate the strength and aggression required by the user in battle. RV

Wedding cape

This cape, made of dyed pandanus leaf, is known as a *kakoto* on Buka Island in the northern Solomons. Such capes are worn by the bride's mother and the bride's father's oldest sister at the wedding ceremony. Towards the end of proceedings the groom removes the cape from each woman, presenting his new in-laws with payments of shell money to legitimise the marriage. The designs are symbolic, and use of the cape is restricted to women of the Peits lineage, the group responsible for tribal peace by acting as messenger and law enforcer. RV

Club (c. 1800), ironwood, L 167.5 x W 12.5 cm

Wedding cape (c. 1880), natural pigments on pandanus leaf, L 115.5 x W 34 cm

Treasures of the Museum

Crocodile mask

Turtle-shell masks, or *karara*, like this one, with the tail of a fish and a head resembling a shark, King Fish or a crocodile, were used in both the Fly River area of Papua New Guinea and the western islands of Torres Strait, from where this mask was collected. They were important characters in the ceremonies of the *horiomo* cult of the dead. Few masks of this kind were made because of the work involved in assembling the turtle shell, cassowary feathers, ovulum shells, pangum seeds and the decorations of white clay and red ochre. Masks were sacred and could be used only by certain male members of a lineage. RV

Bark cloth

Niue is a small island country that, unlike its neighbours Tonga, Samoa and Fiji, appears not to have made *tapa*, or bark cloth, before European contact. Probably in response to tourism, the Niueans began making bark cloth in the early 1880s, when attractive patterns were painted by hand onto cloth produced by pounding together layers of bark strips from the paper mulberry plant. By the turn of the 20th century, this distinctive art form had disappeared. Unlike *tapa* elsewhere in the Pacific, the bark cloth in Niue was too inflexible to have been used as clothing, being more suitable as covers for European tables. RV

Crocodile mask (c. 1850), turtle shell and various decorations, H 54 x L 153 cm

Bark cloth (c. 1890), natural pigments on paper mulberry bark, L 196 x W 196 cm

Indigenous Cultures

Ancestral figure

This carving of a human female figure was made from sacred vesi wood. The feet are attenuated, as if they had been attached to a larger object such as an architectural post. One arm is missing and frequent use has given the figure a distinct patina. The pubic triangle is carved to represent the tattooing every woman of marriageable age was obliged to undertake.

Such images played central roles in Fijian religion, where priests were the medium through which the gods communicated. These ancestral figures, or *matakau*, were material representations of the dead, abodes for spirits from time to time, and were used by priests to communicate with the spirit world. The figures were kept in a spirit house, or *bure kalou*, where they were the last thing captured warriors saw before being put to death and eaten.

Ritual appurtenances were also maintained in the spirit houses. Priests' bowls, or *buburau ni bete*, for drinking kava, the sacred drink of Fiji, were kept here, as well as oil dishes, or *sedre ni waiwai*, from which priests anointed themselves before ceremonies. Equally important were the model spirit houses, made, like the larger ones, almost entirely from coir fibre. Like the ancestral figures kept in the spirit house, miniature whale-tooth ivory figures were kept in the model spirit houses. Both served to assist priests to divine from the gods the proper course of action for their communities. RV

Ancestral figure (c. 1850), vesi wood, H 57.5 x W 16 cm

Treasures of the Museum

Spirit figure

This spirit figure, or *kakame*, is from Kinomere Village in the Gulf Province of Papua New Guinea. These and other figures representing inhabitants of the spirit world are today made for the tourist market. In the past this figure was often used to ward off animals that might interfere with food sources required for ceremonial purposes. Analogous spirits guarded similar ceremonial resources against human predation, while others taught young children about the hazards and products of the bush. RV

Ancestral figure

This figure, from Kamanibit Village on the north coast of Papua New Guinea, was kept in the spirit house where it was given the power to protect the village from unfriendly water spirits called *maselei*. This was especially important during ceremonies when flutes and bull-roarers announced the presence of the paramount spirit of the region's Iatmul people. The main figure is masked and is sitting on a stool with legs made of male and female figures decorated with shell and fibre necklaces, and fibre girdles. RV

Spirit figure (1982), natural pigments on wood, H 101 x W 56 cm

Ancestral figure (c. 1930), wood, shell and natural fibres, H 152 x W 49 cm

Indigenous Cultures

Ceremonial headdress

Each member of the Papua New Guinean Mekeo tribe was born into a patrilineal clan that owned, or was owned by, a particular totem animal or plant. Several ceremonies were conducted each year in which large amounts of assets were passed between clans and sometimes even between tribes. The most important ceremonies were conducted by clan leaders, who wore, as their badges of office, elegant feather headdresses known as *kangakanga*. Each headdress incorporated elements of a clan's totem, perhaps an animal bone, or shell or a particular plant. The central feature of any *kangakanga* was a fretted turtle shell ornament, or *kefe*, a forehead emblem obtained by trade from the Roro people living on the coast. The individual nature of the *kefe*, and the special arrangement of feathers, makes each headdress unique. Feathers in this headdress include those of the bird-of-paradise, cockatoo, parrot and Goura Pigeon. RV

Flute stopper

Like other significant objects of the Iatmul people from the north coast of Papua New Guinea, large bamboo flutes, several metres long, were kept in the spirit house, or *haus tambaran*, where they were seen and used only by initiated men. Flutes are sacred objects and are thought to be the voices of the spirits, low and mellow, always in pairs, the longer one seen as brother, the shorter as sister. This flute stopper, an anthropomorphic figure from the Yuat River, is decorated with valuable objects: cowry shells on the girdle and dogs' teeth forming the necklace. The shells were obtained by barter from coastal areas, and dogs' teeth were regarded as important presentation and ceremonial objects. RV

Headdress (c. 1890), feathers and turtle shell, H 145 x W 85 cm

Flute stopper (c. 1930), bamboo, cowry shells and dogs' teeth, H 92 x W 15.5 cm

Courting mask

Among the Urama in the Gulf of Papua, it is the responsibility of a man to educate the son of his sister, a duty for which he is paid, mainly in pigs and shells, by her husband. Some of the ceremonies acknowledging this responsibility include the birth of the first son, his entry into the longhouse at about two years of age, and marriage. During the courtship leading up to marriage, a secular ritual takes place involving a large figure woven in cane called the *oriho'obo*.

Traditionally, this figure would have been stored in the uninitiated men's longhouse until required, where it would symbolise a man's responsibility to his sister in this sphere of life. Only one *oriho'obo* is made for each lineage; it has a specific and personal lineage name, and its use is restricted to the brother of the lineage leader's wife. In this guise he acts as the agent for all young men in his lineage seeking marriage. The acceptance of a gift proffered by the *oriho'obo* to the young woman's family would formalise the relationship.

This figure was collected from Kinomere Village, where it was made for the museum; similar *oriho'obo* are sometimes for sale to tourists. RV

Courting mask (1982), natural pigments on woven cane, H 215 × W 135 cm

Oriho'obo worn by two Urama men in Tovei Village, Gulf of Papua, 1926
Photographer: Frank Hurley, Australian Museum Collection

Indigenous Cultures

Orator's stool

The centre of an Iatmul village is the spirit house, where objects imbued with spirit are kept, and where men gather to conduct their religion, or simply to gossip and to sleep. This stool, or *teket*, from Kanganaman Village is the seat for the principal ancestral spirit, who authorises village orators to carry on their debates. Each speaker in his turn holds a bunch of sword-like cordyline palm leaves, which he strikes against this seat in calling on the names of the ancestors and emphasising significant points. Such debates are often carried on for hours, underlining the importance attached to this event. RV

Orator's stool (c. 1930), natural pigments on wood, with shells and natural fibres, H 207 x W 68 cm

Treasures of the Museum

House ornament

Ancestral spirits in New Ireland in Papua New Guinea required that the dead be honoured through the construction of memorial *malagan*. This figure is typical of those used in mortuary ceremonies. They were made by specialist carvers under the supervision of clan leaders. The central image is of a hornbill with soaring ear planks flanked by roosters, a design that would have been copyright but which could be sold. Similar *malagan* were made as masks for special ceremonies. Each part of the cycle was accompanied by a public display followed by dancing and feasting. *Malagan* of this type were developed in the 1880s and used perhaps as late as 1931. RV

House ornament (c. 1900), natural pigments on wood, H 156 x W 66.5 cm

Indigenous Cultures

Rambaramp

A man aspiring to prestige and honour on the Vanuatu island of Malekula could have joined one or more of three societies. The most widespread was the Nimangki Society, whose public ceremonies represented a major part of the social, religious and economic life of the island. It had several grades of membership, beginning in childhood and extending through old age. Each grade had its own name and ritual, and members acquired greater esteem with every grade met. The Nalawan Society was more religious and required a year's seclusion in the bush before initiation. The rituals of the highly secret and sacred Nevinbur Society could not be performed in the presence of women, children and uninitiated men, who were warned off by the whirring sound of a bull-roarer.

Against this background of lifelong devotion to acquiring status, elaborate death rituals were performed. Only a man of very high rank could have expected to have been honoured by having an effigy, or *rambaramp*, made of him. The effigy shown here is made of tree fern and wood, and the man's skull is flanked by shoulder branches, each representing a specific grade. The armlet and the faces on the shoulders and the chest design all denote society markings. The hawk's feathers reflect the number of grades achieved through life, and the shell on the left arm was smashed on the forehead of the pig killed in payment for the last ceremony. A prized pig's mandible is on the other arm, showing exaggeratedly re-curved tusks made possible by knocking out the opposing tusks on the upper jaw of a living pig. RV

Rambaramp (c. 1900), fern tree, wood, hawk's feathers, shell, pig's mandible and natural pigments, H 245 x W 87 cm

Treasures of the Museum

Didagur masks

In the Sepik River area of Papua New Guinea, masks are an essential part of the ritual performances of initiation. These male *didagur* masks, representing spirits of the natural world, are worn with a full grass skirt in ceremonies leading to manhood. Here young men undergo rituals in which secret knowledge is revealed and initiates endure tests of courage, strength and stamina. When not in use, the masks are hung in the spirit house, where entry is gained only by those initiated into the secret tribal lore. The Korewori River people, living near the Iatmul heartlands, are well known for their intricate basketry figures. RV

Irawaki figure

Imunu, according to the Urama people in the Gulf of Papua, loosely translates as 'power', and it resides in everything to varying degrees. The greatest expression of this power, *kaia`imunu*, is spiritual, and the most powerful figure representing *kaia`imunu* is *irawaki*. *Kaia`imunu* is the soothsayer for every major decision, whether it be for hunting pigs or crocodiles, or for fighting enemies. When the Urama people call on *kaia`imunu* at the beginning of an expedition, they expect the canoe to be rocked by the *kaia`imunu* spirit residing in *irawaki* as a sign of encouragement. *Kaia`imunu* must also make the fish jump away from the canoe rather than towards it, otherwise the trip is cancelled. RV

1 Mask (1925), natural pigments on woven cane, H 42 x W 45 x L 87 cm
2 Mask (1925), natural pigments on woven cane, H 30 x W 44 x L 73 cm

3 Carved figure (c. 1940), natural pigments on wood and natural fibre, H 184 x W 52 cm

Indigenous Cultures

Feather cloak

Dressed flax, or *whitau*, was finely woven by New Zealand Maori to form mats or cloaks; the item was then often decorated with a border, or *taniko*, of coloured flax – in this case brown and black. The *taniko* was usually woven by men working only in daylight and under a roof. Kiwi feathers could then be attached to the garment, at which time it would be called *kahuhuruhuro kiwi*. To enhance the appearance of the cloak, the base of each feather was knotted with the shaft facing downwards so the feathers fell outwards when the cloak was worn. A few highly treasured red feathers of the parrot, or Kaka, are visible on a part of this cloak.

Like all such treasures, the cloaks were made under *tapu* – strict rules expressed as the wishes of the ancestors. When the cloaks were finished, the *tapu* had to be lifted in order for the cloaks to be safe for anyone to touch or wear. These garments were second only to those made of dog skins, and as such were highly regarded and worn on special occasions and at all ceremonies by individuals of high rank. A feather cloak was also be worn by the groom during a marriage ceremony. RV

Cloak (c. 1900), woven flax, natural pigments and Kiwi and Kaka feathers, L 131 x W 81 cm

Feather box

Traditionally in New Zealand, valuables such as greenstone ornaments or decorative feathers were stored in small, carved boxes called *waka huia*. This one was produced by a highly skilled specialist carver of Te Arawa descent, from the Rotorua region. Such boxes acquired a great deal of spirit, or *tapu*, directly from the carver and later through the prizes held within the box. Maori consider all such *taonga* as living treasures to be regarded with reverence. RV

Birch bark box

Mi`kmaq Native Americans, from the Canadian woodlands of the north-east, decorated their clothing, personal accessories and containers with dyed porcupine quills. This cylindrical birch bark box, used for keeping exchange and personal valuables, is ornamented with quills in a variety of colours. The decoration is traditional, the sides in chevron patterns, while the lid features a cross design with geometric overlays. Native American quill work flourished up until the 18th century, when coloured glass beads became readily available from European traders. Later practices built on the applications and designs of traditional quill work. RV

Box (c. 1900), wood and paua shell, H 13 x W 33 x L 110 cm

Box (1896), birch bark and porcupine quills, H 10.5 x diam. 145 cm

Indigenous Cultures

Totem pole

Among Native American groups on the north-west coast of North America, totem poles are highly visible. Often up to 18 metres high, they are placed in front of the homes of their owners, and many are seen in each village. They are made from single logs of Pacific Coast red cedar.

A man in Haida society has the potential to earn a number of names throughout life for his exploits: as a whale hunter, as a great carver, or as a talented speechmaker, for example. A person who did extremely well would amass names describing his talents, and would attain rights and privileges associated with his status. His fame would be commemorated with a totem pole, his deeds and stories told on the pole through carvings. Such an honour brings with it the need for his family to amass sufficient wealth, often over years, to pay for a first feast due when the log is felled and brought to the village. A second feast occurs when the totem pole is erected.

This 12-metre totem pole, erected at Skidegate Village (British Columbia, Canada), consists of four major carvings representing some of the totems that traditionally travel through the maternal line. From base to top they are Grizzly Bear, Eagle, Killer Whale and Frog. Other figures carved on and around the totems refer to the narratives surrounding the commemoration. The removable segmented cylinder at the top of the pole indicates the number of potlatch feasts given by the owner and his descendants over the life of the pole. It was obtained by the museum in 1911 from the Field Museum of Natural History in Chicago. RV

1

2–3

1 Totem pole at its original site at Skidegate, Skeena, Queen Charlotte Islands, 1901
Source: British Columbia Archives, Canada, I-56088
2 Totem pole (19th century), natural pigments on Pacific Coast red cedar, H 1190 x diam. 120 cm. Main totem shows Eagle, known as 'Hot'
3 The totem Killer Whale, known as 'Sgana'

Dr David Dorward

African textiles

The *rigar kore* (top and bottom left) was a highly valued man's gown, made by Hausa tailors of Kano in northern Nigeria. It was sold to the Kanuri of Borno Kingdom, hundreds of kilometres to the north-east. The gown was made from native cotton woven into five-centimetre strips and sewn together to form a voluminous gown. The hand-embroidery around the collar and on the right breast is traditional Hausa design. The gown was dyed repeatedly with native indigo, soaked in a viscous resin and rubbed with indigo powder before slaves pounded the garment with wooden mallets to create a lustrous sheen.

The *rigar kore* was a prestige item; perspiration or washing would cause the indigo to loose its lustre. Few examples in original condition have survived. This gown is part of a collection of Hausa and Nupe gowns and artefacts from Nigeria, acquired by the museum in 1910 from a British colonial officer, W.H. Freer-Hill.

The toga-like wrapper from which the detail on the bottom right is taken was woven on a narrow loom. The nine-centimetre strips were then sewn together to form the garment. Narrow-strip weaving was well established when European slave traders arrived in West Africa in the 16th century. European textiles, Chinese and (later) Italian silks traded for slaves were unravelled and woven into local garments, employing indigenous designs. In time, the Ashanti (Asante) Kingdom came to dominate the slave trade and the wealth that it generated, which led to royal patronage of weavers and widespread production of prestige cloths. The complexity of design was indicative of the position of the wearer in a hierarchical society. Commonly called *kente* cloth, this example from present-day Ghana is known as *n'tama*. It was purchased from an Ashanti chief in 1893 'for 2 lion's claws and £15 cash'.

Rigar kore (pre-colonial), indigo-dyed cotton, H 131 x W 274 cm
Kente cloth (pre-colonial), cotton and silk, L 268 x W 162 cm
Photographs courtesy of David Dorward

Dr David Dorward

Fertility figure

The pre-colonial grasslands of the western Cameroon comprised numerous ethnically diverse kingdoms that warred with one another in complex, ever-changing alliances. The ceremonial art of the grasslands is prized for its complex symbolism and variety of forms. Such art was not only a public statement of power, the exchange of such items also cemented alliances.

The two major brass-casting centres were at Bamum and Bagam. Before the First World War, brass was costly, traded in from afar. Castings were small: jewellery, brass ceremonial tobacco pipes, and finials on carved drinking horns. Items were moulded in beeswax, which was then encased in a fine slip and covered with coarser layers of clay to build up the mould. The mould was heated to melt the wax, which was replaced by molten metal. Each item was unique, the mould being destroyed to recover the casting. After the Second World War, ready availability of spent brass-shell casings and the development of the African art market increased the size and complexity of grassland brass casting.

This 'mother and child' fertility figure is a fine example of 'contact art', but one that is simultaneously true to grassland artistic traditions and a testament to the sensitivity, stylistic creativity and skills of Bamum brass casters. Near life-size, it was moulded and cast as a single, flawless, three-dimensional piece. It is illustrative of the grasslands love of embellishment: the mother festooned with jewellery, and both mother and child covered with complex designs.

Dr David Dorward is Director of the African Research Institute, LaTrobe University.

Fertility figure (post-1945), brass casting, H 139 x W 36 x D 75 cm

138

Head of mummified female (date unknown), gold leaf on human remains

Coffin of Tamenkhamun (7th century BC), polychrome decoration on wood, lime and plaster, H 40 x W 41 x L 181 cm

Mummy and sarcophagus of Tjeby (1956–1870 BC), human remains with linen, mud and plaster with polychrome decorations, and wood with plaster pigment, H 60 x W 50 x L 210 cm

Dr Colin Hope

Egyptian antiquities

Among the museum's small collection of Mediterranean antiquities are three important items that illustrate how that collection was formed and the perennial fascination with ancient Egyptian attempts to preserve the body to ensure eternal life after death.

The well-preserved human head is one of a number of body parts undoubtedly brought to Australia as mementoes of visits to Egypt. The difficulty of transporting complete mummies resulted in the dismembering of bodies and the acquisition of parts, especially heads. A reference to a head with attached gold foil, in a letter to Redmond Barry dated 14 May 1856, suggests this head might have come from Maxamillian Weidenbach, one of two brothers who had acted as artists for Egyptologist R. Lepsius. The traces of gold foil reflect the belief that survival in the next life could be enhanced through identification with the gods, whose skin was of gold.

In 1925, the mummy and coffin of Tjeby the Elder arrived in Melbourne, having been donated by Alan Rowe in 1923. Rowe, who came to Australia early in the 20th century, joined G. Reisner's excavation team in Egypt in 1922. As a result of his contribution, Reisner gave this mummy and coffin to Rowe, who donated them to the museum. Tjeby was discovered in the cemetery of Sheikh Farag, in southern Egypt, in a small, undecorated tomb in which another man, also named Tjeby, was also buried; they were probably father and son. His body was wrapped in linen, his chest covered with plaster painted with a floral collar, and his head covered with mud modelled to show his facial features and the wig he would have worn during life. The coffin and its lid carry hieroglyphic inscriptions requesting an eternal supply of offerings from the gods. Tjeby lived during the second part of the 20th century BC to the early part of the 19th century BC; he is the oldest ancient Egyptian in Australia. His cause of death is unknown; his teeth are much worn and he suffered from dental caries and abscesses. His body is intact, and there are no traces of evisceration or attempts to remove the brain, practices aimed at preventing internal decay damaging the body.

The decorated wooden coffin of Tamenkhamun is the only significant Egyptian antiquity to enter the collection in recent times. It was acquired from the collection of J. Bedford, postmaster at Kyancutta in South Australia, who also established a small museum. Bedford purchased the coffin in England in 1910 and it was sold in the 1960s, well after his death. Inscriptions on the coffin note that Tamenkhamun was a 7th century BC minor official in the administration of property owned by the temple of the god Amun at Thebes. The coffin's decoration is shown as though upon the bandages of the body itself, and comprises representations of various gods who ensured the protection of the body. It also shows a figure of the mummified body lying upon a lion bed with the soul shown as a bird hovering above and Tamenkhamun himself making offerings to the gods. On the basal section is the standard of Osiris, god of resurrection. The inscriptions contain prayers to the gods and the request for an eternal supply of offerings for Tamenkhamun.

Dr Colin Hope is Director of the Centre for Archaeology and Ancient History at Monash University and a research associate of the museum. He specialises in the archaeology of ancient Egypt and north-eastern Africa, from late prehistoric times until the advent of Christianity.

Trilobite (see page 168)

Sciences

Standardwing (*Semioptera wallacei*)

Sciences

John Gould

'The Bird Man', Englishman John Gould (1804–81), was an apprenticed gardener who became a taxidermist, natural history dealer, accomplished author and ornithologist. He published numerous scientific articles and 43 volumes of natural history. These were lavishly illustrated with 3100 hand-coloured lithographs. Gould's wife, Elizabeth, prepared the initial sketches and then transferred them to stone engravings. She also completed the initial hand-colourings.

The Goulds completed major works for several continents before turning to the natural history of the new Australian colonies. This was an uncharted area, and John Gould's initial attempts were thwarted by a lack of information. The ambitious project commenced with a visit to Australia between 1838 and 1840. Government offices provided accommodation and facilities, and field workers were employed, one of whom was John Gilbert.

Much of the material acquired on this visit was undescribed and subsequently named by Gould. Shortly after returning to England, Elizabeth died tragically. Gould then relied on other artists to complete his works based on his rough sketches. Henry Richter (1821–1902) was one such artist. He prepared 595 lithographs for Gould's seven-volume *The Birds of Australia*.

This watercolour painting of a Southern Cassowary was painted by Henry Richter, and outlines the composition and colours to be used for the lithographic process. The lithographs were then hand-coloured by a team of artists using 'pattern plates' as guides, which indicated what colours to use and where. The completed lithograph derived from this watercolour appeared in the *Supplement to the Birds of Australia*, published in London between 1851 and 1869.

Indonesia's Standardwing is an unusual bird-of-paradise. The male has a remarkable white feather plume extending from the wrist of each wing, giving the bird its popular name. These plumes are used as part of the species' spectacular mating display and are manoeuvred like banners. The species is restricted to the northern Moluccas, where it was discovered by Alfred Russel Wallace. The Standardwing was described in 1859 by John Gould and named in honour of its discoverer. Specimens in the museum's collection are part of the material collected by Wallace and later purchased from Gould. They are some of the first-known specimens of the species and could be part of the original material seen by Gould while writing his description. NWL & RO'B

Henry Richter, Southern Cassowary (*Casuarius casuarius*), watercolour, H 68 x W 86 cm

Treasures of the Museum

Alfred Russel Wallace

Alfred Russel Wallace (1823–1913) was an explorer and scientist best known for his ideas on natural selection and the theory of evolution. In some respects, Wallace is thought of as a 'forgotten naturalist', overshadowed by the success of Charles Darwin. Initially a teacher, Wallace left England to travel in South America's Amazon region and later throughout South-East Asia. He was an astute scientist with a wonderful feeling for natural history and a keen zoological eye. During his travels, he procured massive natural history collections, many for the British Museum. These included 2474 specimens of birds and 123 of mammals from the Indonesian Archipelago. Other vertebrate specimens were destined for the then infant National Museum of Victoria. These were obtained by the museum's director, Frederick McCoy, from John Gould, to whom they had been forwarded for resale. Many of the specimens are retained by the museum as scientific study-skins; others are mounted and have at times been placed on public display.

Like Gould and Darwin, Alfred Wallace was a prolific author. His writings were well researched and are as valuable and interesting today as they were when they were first published. One of his major publications, written jointly in 1858 with Charles Darwin, appeared in the *Journal of the Linnean Society of London* and considered the idea of natural selection. This cooperative work was an effort to expand on information Wallace had published previously, in 1856, in the *Annals and Magazine of Natural History*. Other publications reflected his ideas and findings through his researches in the Indo-Malayan and Indonesian archipelagos.

1 Dusky Lory (*Pseudeos fuscata*)
2 Red Bird-of-Paradise (*Paradisea rubra*)

Sciences

Among the birds collected in the Indonesian archipelago were many birds-of-paradise. One, the Red Bird-of-Paradise, is an inhabitant of rainforests of the western Papuan islands of Indonesia. Its spectacularly coloured flank plumes give the bird its common name. John Gould considered the bird to have great artistic appeal, and subsequent popular reproductions of his works regularly include this species. After obtaining the specimen from Wallace, Gould sold it to the museum as part of a larger series of zoological specimens.

Another of Alfred Wallace's specimens received from John Gould was the Dusky Lory, a species of parrot from New Guinea and Indonesia. The specimen obtained belongs to a subspecies confined to the Indonesian islands of Japen and Salawati. It is smaller than its mainland counterpart. Wallace would have first encountered this bizarrely plumaged parrot in lowland forests and woodlands. Dusky Lories have highly variable colouration. The red, yellow and dusky brown plumage varies across the bird's range; in some areas the red dominates while in other areas the yellow or dusky brown does. NWL

145

Charles Darwin

Charles Darwin (1809–82) is best known for his theory of evolution. Initially persuaded by his father to train as a physician, Darwin instead turned to the clergy. He joined HMS *Beagle* as an unpaid naturalist and, over five years, sailed around the world.

Observations made during this voyage led him to re-evaluate biodiversity and to question the mechanisms underlying the variety of species. Evidence for his theory of evolution included differences he observed between the finches on the Galapagos Islands off Ecuador. Each island was inhabited by a unique species remarkably adapted to its particular environment and way of life.

In 1858, Darwin co-authored with Alfred Russel Wallace a scientific article on evolution. Their thesis challenged accepted beliefs about creation, but it was Darwin's expansion of these ideas in *On the Origin of Species by Means of Natural Selection* (1859) that set in train general acceptance of the theory initially given a hostile reception in some quarters.

The museum possesses three specimens collected in South America by Darwin during the voyage of HMS *Beagle*. Two birds were sent to Melbourne between 1858 and 1869 by John Gould. The Great Pampa-Finch had been well prepared and conserved but it lacks its tail. This specimen was obtained at Maldanado, Uruguay; a second bird, the Grassland Sparrow, was also from Uruguay. The Southern Mountain Cavy, a kind of guinea pig, was collected by Darwin in Patagonia in 1837. NWL

Great Pampa-Finch (*Embernagra platensis*)

Southern Mountain Cavy (*Microcavia australis*)

Sciences

William Blandowski

The first zoologist hired to develop collections for the museum was the controversial William Blandowski (1822–78). A German, with interests and experience in natural history, Blandowski collected vigorously throughout Victoria. His best-known trip was a poorly planned expedition to the junction of the Murray and Darling rivers in 1856–57, during which five of his six assistants deserted him. Although more than 17 000 specimens were collected, only about a third exist today in museums. Many specimens requiring taxidermy in the field were destroyed by insects, others were kept by Blandowski himself, and still others were later exchanged.

Blandowski attempted to publish descriptions of fish species he had collected, naming several after prominent members of the council of the Philosophical Institute – later, the Royal Society of Victoria. Blandowski's motivation for recognising the council members was apparent in uncomplimentary descriptions accompanying his accounts of purported new species. *Brosmius bleasdalii*, named after the Reverend Mr Bleasdale, was described as a 'slimy, slippery fish' that 'lives in the mud', while *Cernua eadesii*, 'honouring' Dr Eades, was portrayed as 'a fish easily recognized by its low forehead, big belly and sharp spine'. An editorial in the *Argus* declared that Dr Eades considered Mr Blandowski's description to attack 'peculiarities in the conformation of the Doctor's frontal and abdominal regions'. Public objections from council members resulted in the removal of the article from the issue prior to its binding. The scandal forced Blandowski to return to Hamburg, taking with him notes, drawings and many of the specimens from the expedition. There, he protested his unfair treatment in the colony.

In his failed publication, Blandowski described what he thought were four new species of fish. These are likely to have been based on four individuals of Silver Perch. The Blandowski specimen shown overleaf

closely resembles his figure of *Cernua bidyana*. It is likely Blandowski's *C. eadesii*, was based on a large and very pregnant specimen of Silver Perch. Unfortunately, none of the specimens currently in the museum matches Blandowski's figures, and it is probable that his figured specimens returned to Europe with him.

The Trout Cod is one of the few Australian fishes considered endangered by the International Union for the Conservation of Nature. It was once abundant and widespread in the Murray and Darling rivers, where Blandowski collected, but degradation of aquatic habitats has resulted in a serious decline of Trout Cod populations. Today, the only remaining self-sustaining wild populations are found in short sections of the Murray and Goulburn rivers in northern Victoria. The specimen shown overleaf, like most of Blandowski's fishes, is a dry skin from one side of the fish.

The Lesser Stick-nest Rat inhabited samphire shrub land, where it built large stick-nests. It was nocturnal, feeding on succulent vegetation. The species had become extinct in Victoria by the late 1920s and throughout Australia by 1933, probably as a result of competition for grazing by introduced stock. The results from the Blandowski Expedition contributed a little knowledge about the biology of this species before its extinction.

The Pig-footed Bandicoot was collected from north-western Victoria and first described in 1836 by Sir Thomas Mitchell. The Blandowski Expedition collected a specimen in 1857, across the Murray River, in New South Wales. The bandicoot was noted by one member of the expedition, Gerard Krefft, as becoming scarce in areas where it grazed. It became extinct in this area in the 1860s but lasted until 1907 in Central Australia. It is believed that competition for grazing by introduced stock hastened its extinction. Very little of the biology of this species was ever recorded. MG & RO'B

1

2

Sciences

3

4

1 Silver Perch (*Bidyanus bidyanus*)
2 Trout Cod (*Maccullochella macquariensis*)
3 Pig-footed Bandicoot (*Chearopus ecaudatus*)
4 Lesser Stick-nest Rat (*Leporillus apicalis*)

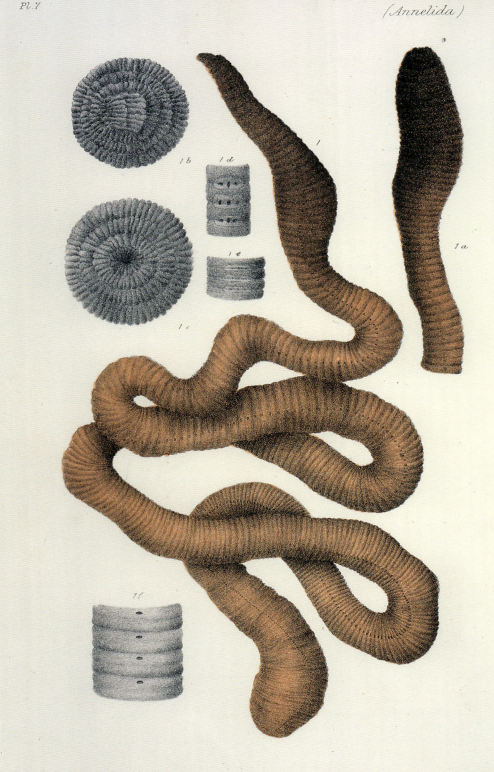

Giant Gippsland Earthworm (*Megascolides australis*). Arthur Bartholomew's lithograph in the *Prodromus of the Zoology of Victoria*, decade 1, plate 7 (1879) and one of the earliest specimens collected

Sciences

Frederick McCoy
and his Prodromus

Frederick McCoy (c. 1823–99) joined the University of Melbourne as Professor of Natural Science in 1855 and became the director of the museum in 1858. McCoy made many contributions to science in the new colony, especially in the fields of zoology, stratigraphy and palaeontology.

In 1874, McCoy began publication of his *Prodromus of the Zoology of Victoria* and *Prodromus of the Palaeontology of Victoria*. The two volumes of 200 zoological plates and one volume of 70 palaeontological plates set out to be 'systematic publications . . . as might be useful and interesting to the general public and contribute to the advancement of science'. Publication of the plates in sets of 10, called 'decades', continued until 1890 but were never reissued in systematic order as had been intended. Each plate is a lithograph made from drawings by the artists Ludwig Becker, Edward Gilkes, Arthur Bartholomew, James Ripper and John Wild. Initially, the lithographs for the zoological *Prodromus* were printed in black and white and were then hand-coloured, but later editions were printed in colour. McCoy made a special effort in the case of the living species to have the drawings done from fresh specimens so that the colours and appearance were as natural as possible. Many of the specimens from which the drawings were made remain in the museum's collection today.

The Giant Gippsland Earthworm is larger than most other species of earthworm and could be the longest in the world. The length of a worm is difficult to determine, but when fully expanded, the Gippsland species is reported to reach four metres. A less exaggerated estimate is 1.5 metres. These gigantic worms were discovered by surveyors in the Brandy Creek region of Gippsland, Victoria, and sent to McCoy, who recognised them

as a new species. The specimen illustrated in Arthur Bartholomew's lithograph might no longer exist; the actual worm studied and described by McCoy in 1879 exists in fragments in the museum collection. The earthworm survives in a few valleys near Warragul and Korumburra. Its ecology is similar to that of other earthworms, only on a bigger scale – it burrows to four metres deep by eating earth.

The Murray Spiny Crayfish (*Euastacus armatus*) was drawn by Ludwig Becker and labelled *Astacopsis serratus*. This genus name is now restricted to crayfish from Tasmania, and the species name is predated by another, *armatus*, introduced in 1866 by the German biologist Eduard von Martens. The specimen drawn for the *Prodromus* is the largest known at 32 centimetres long. Although the species can still be found in the Murray River and its tributaries, it is no longer 'very common' as McCoy reported, and fishing has ensured that none this big remains today. McCoy's interest in the crayfish was perhaps stimulated by the 'considerable quantity' sent to the Melbourne market. The museum now houses an extensive collection of about 90 species of freshwater crayfish and yabbies from south-eastern Australia.

The giant fossil cowry was first described and named by McCoy in 1867, and illustrated in 1875 and 1876 in decades two and three of the *Prodromus of the Palaeontology of Victoria*. The specimen shown overleaf, and drawn by Arthur Bartholomew, was found in strata of Middle Miocene age (approximately 15 million years old) near Hamilton, western Victoria. The species also occurs in beds of the same age at Mornington, Batesford near Geelong, Princetown near Port Campbell, and in East Gippsland, and a closely related species occurs in older beds at Torquay. It is the largest known cowry,

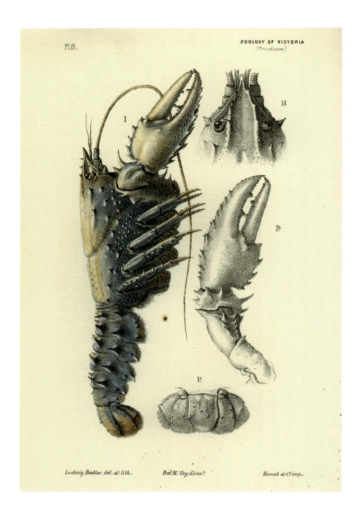

either fossil or living, reaching a length of more than 22 centimetres. Living cowries reach only about half this size. Although other giant fossil cowries are known from Europe and Asia, these are not related to the Australian fossils and they are older.

The Bramble Shark (*Echinorhinus brucus*) is a sluggish, deep-water species taken only occasionally by commercial fishing trawlers at depths of 400 metres and more. McCoy recognised its rarity, reporting a specimen of 'Spinous Shark' caught off Portland in 1886, and he illustrated it in his *Prodromus* as the first record of the species from Australia. Gilbert Whitley, a prodigious describer of fishes working at the Australian Museum in Sydney, decided McCoy's specimen represented a new species and in 1931 named it for him – *Echinorhinus* (*Rubosqualus*) *mccoyi*. Today, experts consider McCoy's identification to be correct. The differences noted by Whitley are attributable to either Bartholomew's published figure or peculiarities of the mounted specimen. Nevertheless, the specimen remains the type for Whitley's now rejected species name. GP, DJH & MG

Murray Spiny Crayfish (*Euastacus armatus*). Ludwig Becker's lithograph in the *Prodromus of the Zoology of Victoria,* decade 2, plate 15 (1879) and the specimen from which it was drawn

Sciences

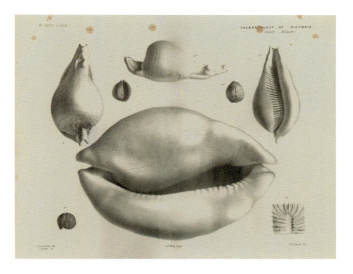 

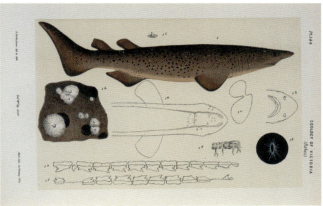 

Giant fossil cowry (*Gigantocypraea gigas*). Arthur Bartholomew's lithograph (main shell) in the *Prodromus of the Palaeontology of Victoria*, decade 3, plates 28–29 (1876) and the specimen from which it was drawn alongside a modern cowry (*Umbilia hesitata*) of typical size

Bramble Shark (*Echinorhinus brucus*). Arthur Bartholomew's lithograph in the *Prodromus of the Zoology of Victoria*, decade 15, plate 144 (1887) and the specimen from which it was drawn, the type of *Echinorhinus* (*Rubosqualus*) *mccoyi*

Walter Baldwin Spencer and the Horn Expedition

In 1894, William Augustus Horn, a wealthy South Australian pastoralist and miner, organised an exploration of Central Australia. The Victorian government commissioned Walter Baldwin Spencer (1860–1929), Professor of Biology at the University of Melbourne, to participate as the expedition zoologist. Spencer not only joined the group on its arduous journey but also edited a major publication on its results. The Horn Expedition collected animals of all sorts for the museum, including numerous rarely encountered species. These collections were supplemented by material supplied by local landholders. Many of the species represented are now considered extinct or threatened, making the examples from the expedition a unique resource for research and education.

Several authors published their findings on the expedition's vertebrate collections in research journals and in the four volumes edited by Spencer. Under agreement, the expedition's specimens were dispersed across several institutions; 19 birds were sent to the British Museum (Natural History), but many mammals were deposited in Victoria's museum.

Spencer and E.R. Waite examined the mammals obtained by the Horn Expedition. Spencer described five new taxa: the Fat-tailed False Antechinus, the Sandhill Dunnart, the Kowari, the Stripe-faced Dunnart (through individual variation in the species the Stripe-faced Dunnart received two names; these two animals are now correctly identified as belonging to the same taxon). Waite was especially interested in rodents, describing three new species: the Central Rock Rat, the Shark Bay Mouse and the Sandy Inland Mouse.

The museum's specimen of the Spinifex Hopping Mouse was originally retained by Spencer at his university office and not received at the museum until two decades later. The species was not recognised as new until 1922.

Today, the carnivorous Mulgara is considered to be vulnerable in its arid habitats. The museum's specimen is an adult male collected at Charlotte Waters, where the species was regarded as common in 1894. NWL & RO'B

Mulgara (*Dasycercus cristicauda*)
Skull of the Spinifex Hopping Mouse (*Notomys alexis*)

Sciences

1–3

Donald Thomson

Like his mentor Walter Baldwin Spencer, Donald Thomson (1901–70) was highly regarded as an anthropologist. Although basing himself in Melbourne, Thomson determined at an early age to participate in expeditions, and these eventually established his scientific reputation. Major expeditions to Cape York Peninsula, Queensland (1928–29 and 1932), and Arnhem Land, Northern Territory (1935, 1936–37 and 1941–43), resulted in a wealth of information.

Thomson also had an early interest in natural history, and he obtained more than 300 bird specimens, 400 mammals and more than 700 fish specimens during his expeditions. Before Thomson's expeditions, little faunal material from the northern regions of Australia was available. Thomson's meticulous notes provide good detail that helps researchers to understand the species' ecology and populations. Each specimen was cross-referenced to native names and its relevance to Indigenous culture. Many of his specimens are from species today regarded as threatened, such as the Golden-shouldered Parrot and the Cape York Peninsula population of the Brush-tailed Phascogale.

Thomson obtained a male of the Northern Quoll from Trial Bay in the Northern Territory in 1942, where it was regarded as numerous. Due to encroachment by the Cane Toad, native animals such as this species may one day become threatened.

The Northern Hopping Mouse is restricted to coastal regions of the Northern Territory and to Groote Eylandt but is not considered threatened. Thomson's specimen of a female was collected on Groote Eylandt.

His specimen of the unusual Rough Knob-tailed Gecko was collected in 1933 near the Lower Archer River, Cape York, Queensland. NWL

1 Skull of the Northern Quoll (*Dasyurus hallucatus*)
2 Skull of the Northern Hopping Mouse (*Notomys aquilo*)
3 Rough Knob-tailed Gecko (*Nephurus asper*)

Alfred William Howitt

English-born Alfred William Howitt (1830–1908) was a leading light in Victorian natural history and anthropology. He was an energetic explorer and bushman who travelled widely throughout Victoria and the arid interior. Howitt was chosen to locate the expedition of Burke and Wills in September 1862. Funded through government subscription, he travelled to the expedition depot on Cooper Creek in South Australia. After finding the sole remaining member of the ill-fated trip, he returned to Melbourne. Two months later, Howitt returned to Cooper Creek seeking the remains of Burke and Wills, but also with the objective of investigating selections for grazing. Without the pressures of searching for lost expedition members, Howitt found time to explore the natural history of the area. It is presumed that during this second trip, Howitt collected 24 bird specimens and two mammals. There is no actual evidence the mammal specimens were from the Cooper Creek area; however, each bird specimen is tagged with a label reporting that it was collected on 'Howitt's Cooper Creek Expedition'.

The White-winged Fairy-wren is confined to dry environments and it occurs in various colour intensities across its range. The cobalt blue of Howitt's specimen typifies the populations of the arid interior. There, they frequent lignum swamps or areas of grassland interspersed with low, open shrubs.

The provenance of Howitt's two specimens of the White-footed Rabbit Rat is uncertain. This now extinct species is not known to have occured in the Cooper Creek drainage, although the museum's specimen register lists both specimens as coming from that area. Howitt mentioned the species in his accounts of eastern Gippsland fauna but there is no definite proof that the museum's material came from either locality. NWL

Mandible and skull of the White-footed Rabbit Rat (*Conilurus albipes*)
Male White-winged Fairy-wren (*Malurus leucopterus*)

Sciences

H.L. White Collection of Australian Birds' Eggs

Henry Luke White's (1860–1927) collection of Australian birds' eggs remains the finest of its type, with most native bird species represented. The collection contains 4200 clutches, totalling 13 000 eggs.

White was a wealthy pastoralist who lived at Belltrees near Scone, New South Wales. His passion for collecting Australian birds' eggs began as a boyhood hobby and continued throughout his life. Between 1907 and 1909, White significantly increased his own collection by purchasing others from friends Sidney Jackson and Dudley Le Souef. From about 1904, he employed field collectors to travel throughout Australia collecting birds' eggs and bird skins. In 1917, he donated his collection of 8850 study-skins to the museum to be used by members of the Royal Australasian Ornithologists' Union, a club based in Melbourne.

The collection was at one stage intended to go to the Australian Museum in Sydney, but White had a personal antipathy to the then curator of birds, Alfred North. The White collection is significant for its coverage of species, its displays of egg variation and for the data on breeding biology associated with each collection. One extinct species of Australian bird is represented – the Paradise Parrot, collected in 1896 from Queensland. RO'B

Eggs of the Australian Magpie (*Gymnorhina tibicen*)

H.L. White's eggs in the Queensland Maple storage cabinet in which they were donated

Margaret Cameron

Treasures from the museum library

The museum library has many functions, including being a reference collection to support the work of researchers and a repository for archival material and books. The materials it contains – many of which are rare – are as much a part of the museum's intellectual capital as the physical objects and researchers who work on them.

J.J. Halley's *Monograph of the Psittacidae, or Parrot Family of Australia* is considered the most rare Australian bird and colour-plate book produced in Australia. Only three other copies are known: one in the Mitchell Library, Sydney, and two in private collections. Published by the author in Ballarat in 1871, the monograph is the first part of a work that was to be issued in 10 parts. The project failed due to insufficient subscribers. The Sulphur-crested Cockatoo shown here is depicted in a drawing room, and Halley's rather more popular than scientific text describes the bird's habits when domesticated – 'They . . . will climb up a lady's dress and nestle in her neck and bosom, and with their strong beaks take a gentle kiss' – as well as when in the wild. He includes his observations of the bird being hunted by Aboriginal people of the Lower Murray. James W. Sayer drew each bird and Richard Laishley contributed to lithography in the book. Laishley exhibited illustrations intended for the book at the 1870 Sydney Intercolonial Exhibition.

Field notes of John Cotton

Descriptive Chart of Common Insectivorous Birds of Victoria, produced by the government in 1878 for Victorian state schools

Sulphur-crested Cockatoo (*Cacatua galerita*), the frontispiece to J.J. Halley's *Monograph of the Psittacidae, or Parrot Family of Australia* (1871)

Also notable for his amateur ornithological work during the early years of colonisation is John Cotton, many of whose manuscripts are held in the museum. Cotton was born in England in 1802 and emigrated to Australia in 1843. Near Cape Otway on 11 May 1843, he noted that 'a little bird with a flame red breast flew . . . towards the land'; this was probably the first record of the Flame Robin's migration between Tasmania and mainland Australia. Cotton's diaries and his letters to his brother William in England include many observations of local birdlife and were illustrated with detailed sketches. Given the changes that have occurred since settlement, these documents provide useful evidence of the effect of ecological change.

Another rare item the museum holds is the *Descriptive Chart of Common Insectivorous Birds found in Victoria*. It was prepared in the Department of Agriculture in 1878 for use in state schools, and its illustrations were taken from the original drawings of John Cotton, and from Gould's *Birds of Australia*. It shows 36 species of insectivorous birds indigenous to Victoria, gives the diet and distribution of each and declares that these birds 'will be protected by law from destruction'. Sadly, a number of the birds are no longer common and some, including the Hooded Robin and the Scarlet Robin, are becoming rare in Victoria.

A keen birdwatcher, Margaret Cameron, AM, D.Univ, was a member of the council of Museum Victoria from 1987 to 1996. She has been University Librarian (1977–96) and Pro Vice Chancellor (1986–90) of Deakin University, and the president of the Royal Australasian Ornithologists Union (1986–89), of which she is a fellow.

David Holmes Collection of Butterflies and Moths

One of David Holmes' lasting memories of his time in New Guinea during the Second World War was of the magnificent butterfly fauna. When he returned to Australia, he took up butterfly and moth collecting, which soon became his passion.

David Holmes and his wife, Joyce, ran a fruit orchard at Red Hill, south of Melbourne, for more than 40 years. Each year they would take their children on trips to various parts of Australia to collect butterflies. Holmes also swapped, traded and purchased overseas specimens from dealers and other avid collectors. His is the most extensive private butterfly collection in Australia; as an indication of its scope, it contains specimens of every swallowtail butterfly species in North America.

Holmes recently donated his butterfly and moth collection to the museum. To him it represents a lifetime of pleasure and personal rewards, and to the museum it represents an irreplaceable insect collection. KW

John Curtis Collection of Insects

In 1863, Frederick McCoy, director of the museum, purchased the John Curtis Collection of British and Foreign Insects for £567. John Curtis (1791–1862) was a well-known British entomologist who amassed a collection of over 40 000 specimens, covering all major orders of insects and containing many type specimens used to describe new species. The specimens in the collection were gathered either by Curtis himself or by other eminent British entomologists of the day. The oldest specimen dates back to 1796.

McCoy also purchased the Curtis Agricultural Insect Collection, which documents British agricultural pest insects. This is an invaluable biological snapshot of British insect pest fauna from the 1820s to 1860s. Curtis maintained handwritten diaries that detail the locality and host records for every specimen in the collection. It continues to be examined by British and American scientists today because the type specimens of many British species are included. It also contains species now considered to be extinct in England. KW

Moth specimens, David Holmes Collection

Wasp drawer, John Curtis Collection

Treasures of the Museum

Koonwarra fossil bed

The Koonwarra fossil bed of South Gippsland, Victoria, has been described as 'one of the great fossil localities of the Mesozoic Era'. The site was discovered in 1961 by workmen who were straightening a bend in the South Gippsland Highway near Koonwarra, 142 kilometres from Melbourne. The locality has yielded abundant fossils of fishes, plants and insects, exquisitely preserved in thinly layered mudstones deposited in a freshwater lake about 115 million years ago, during the Early Cretaceous Period. The insects include mayflies, dragonflies, cockroaches, beetles, fleas, flies and wasps. Most of these belong to families still alive today, demonstrating the antiquity of the modern Australian insect fauna. The plants include ferns, conifers, relatives of the modern *Ginkgo*, and possible flowering plants that are among the oldest known in the world. Also present are crustaceans, spiders, possible earthworms, bird feathers and a horseshoe crab. The feathers represent one of the oldest known fossil records of birds.

The Koonwarra site is important scientifically because of the large number of species present, their excellent preservation, and the information they provide on the environment in which they lived. At this time, Australia was still attached to Antarctica, and was situated much farther south than at present, placing southern Victoria in the polar region. The evidence provided by the fossils is consistent with a very cold climate. Some of the insects are similar to forms living today in cool mountain streams and lakes in alpine or subalpine areas, and the abundance of fish indicates that they were killed in large numbers, possibly due to the surface of the lake freezing in winter.   DJH

1

2

3–4

1 Fish (*Wadeichthys oxyops*)
2 Flea (*Tarwinia australis*)
3 Water treader or true bug (*Duncanovelia extensa*)
4 Feather

Sciences

F.A. Cudmore Collection of Tertiary Fossils

The Tertiary is the relatively recent interval of Earth's history between 65 million and 1.78 million years ago. Sedimentary rocks of Tertiary age are widespread in south-eastern Australia, and the museum houses the largest and most representative collections of fossils from these rocks in the country. These fossils are usually better preserved than those in older rocks because they are less altered by mineral replacement and have not been deformed by forces deep in the Earth's crust.

A major source of the Tertiary fossils in the museum has been from private collections, many acquired during the early part of the 20th century. The most important of these, and one of the finest of its type, is the vast collection of F.A. Cudmore (1892–1956), which was donated in 1937. As well as molluscs, such as gastropods (snails), bivalves (mussels, clams) and scaphopods (tusk shells), his collection also includes corals, sea urchins, crustaceans and sharks' teeth. The specimens come from Victoria, Tasmania and South Australia.

Cudmore began collecting fossils while still a schoolboy, and he regularly donated specimens to the museum as early as 1904. He was appointed an honorary associate of the museum in 1931, and was also briefly employed as acting palaeontologist in 1934. In addition to his fossil collecting, he was an active member of the Royal Society of Victoria and the Field Naturalists' Club of Victoria. DJH

1–2

3–5

6–8

1 Crab (*Ommatocarcinus corioensis*), Middle Miocene
(c. 11–14 million years old), Barwon River, Victoria

2 Gastropod (*Tenagodus occlusus*), Morgan Limestone, Middle Miocene
(c. 15 million years old), Murray River cliffs, South Australia

3 Volute (*Ternivoluta antiscalaris*), Middle Miocene
(c. 15 million years old), Mt Eliza, Victoria

4 Cone shell (*Conus ligatus*), Middle Miocene
(c. 15 million years old), Mornington, Victoria

5 Gastropod (*Tylospira coronata*), Late Miocene
(c. 5 million years old), near Lakes Entrance, Victoria

6 Sea urchin (*Cyclaster archeri*), Early Miocene
(c. 15–17 million years old), Morgan, South Australia

7 Cowry (gastropod; *Nototrivia avellanoides*), Middle Miocene
(c. 15 million years old), Mornington, Victoria

8 Bivalve (*Tucetona convexa*), Dry Creek Sands, Late Miocene
(c. 8 million years old), Adelaide, South Australia

Graptolites

Graptolites are an extinct group of animals that were once widely distributed in the oceans. They formed twig-like colonies composed of one or more branches that mostly floated freely in the surface waters, though some were attached to the sea floor. Because of their branching form they superficially resembled seaweed, but they were in fact animals. Each branch of a colony housed many individual microscopic animals joined by a type of nerve system. Graptolites first appeared about 500 million years ago and died out about 315 million years ago.

Graptolites are not visually impressive fossils. The flattened remains of their colonies tend to resemble pencil marks on the rock, and the name 'graptolite' is derived from the Greek words meaning 'writing on stone'. However, their unimpressive appearance is not indicative of their scientific significance, as they are one of the most useful groups of fossils for dating rocks worldwide, particularly rocks deposited during the Ordovician, Silurian and early part of the Devonian periods. The Ordovician rocks of central and eastern Victoria contain one of the richest and most diverse assemblages of graptolite faunas in the world, and the extensive collections of these faunas in the museum are of international importance. The Victorian graptolite faunas have been used to subdivide the local Ordovician sequences into 30 intervals and to correlate these intervals accurately with other sequences in New Zealand, Asia, Europe and North America. Graptolites have also been used to work out the structure and sequence of rocks in the central Victorian goldfields, as the strata themselves are too uniform in appearance to enable this to be done on the basis of rock type. DJH

1 Two specimens of *Pendeograptus fruticosus*

2 Two specimens of *Climacograptus bicornis*

3 *Sigmagraptus crinitus* with *Phyllograptus* or *Pseudophyllograptus*

4 *Didymograptus caduceus*

5 Two specimens of *Rhabdinopora scitulum*

6 *Clonograptus persistens*

Sciences

Diprotodon

Diprotodon, the largest marsupial that ever lived, looked somewhat like a long-legged wombat. It occurred over most of Australia, apart from in the extreme south-west and in Tasmania.

Most examples of the skulls of this animal have been crushed in the fossilisation process because they are remarkably thin compared to those of similar-sized mammals such as the rhinoceros. Rare exceptions are found in the museum's collection from Bacchus Marsh, where unusual preservation provides information about internal structure as well as external form. The internal structure shows that *Diprotodon* evolved unique ways to minimise the weight of the skull and the amount of bone that was necessary to form it, factors that might have given it a competitive edge in surviving in a nutrient-poor environment. TR

Zygomaturus

The large marsupial *Zygomaturus* was restricted to south-eastern and south-western Australia, unlike its close relative the more widely ranging *Diprotodon*. This reflects the preference of *Zygomaturus* for lush, forested habitats in contrast to the open plains and arid regions favoured by *Diprotodon*. The two were four-footed herbivores that might have overlapped in their dietary preferences with the larger kangaroos. Competition with the kangaroos for food might have contributed to the extinction of *Zygomaturus* and *Diprotodon*. This skeleton was donated to the museum early in the 20th century by the Queen Victoria Museum and Art Gallery in Launceston, Tasmania. Staff from that museum collected this specimen from Mowbray Swamp near Smithton, Tasmania, a *Zygomaturus* graveyard that has produced the most complete skeletons of this animal. TR

Diprotodon (marsupial) skull, Pleistocene
(1.8 million–10 000 years old), Bacchus Marsh, Victoria

Zygomaturus (diprotodontid marsupial), Pleistocene
(1.8 million–10 000 years old), Mowbray Swamp, Tasmania

Treasures of the Museum

Victorian dinosaurs and fossil mammals

Half the known dinosaurs found in Victoria are hypsilophodontids, which superficially resembled kangaroos but are more distantly related to them than we humans are. Australia was further south 115 million years ago than it is today, and was joined to Antarctica. Because hypsilophodontids were particularly well adapted to the conditions, they thrived in what was then polar south-eastern Australia. The area of their brains processing light from the eyes, the optic lobes, had become enlarged to such an extent that hypsilophodontids may have been able to see and remain active even during winter when the sun did not rise for weeks or months at a time. We think this because the tiny skull has enlarged optic lobes, and cross-sections of its bones are without the patterns that might indicate hibernation.

Mammals that lived alongside the dinosaurs in Victoria were extremely tiny. The pictured jaw, only 16 millimetres long, was a surprise when found because it appears to belong to the placental mammals – those that bear their young at an advanced stage of development. More than twice as old as the oldest known marsupial from Australia, these mammals were previously thought to have reached this continent long after marsupials. For this reason, this jaw is not widely accepted by palaeontologists as that of a placental mammal. Being so highly contentious makes it a most important fossil. TR

Ausktribosphenos Nyktos jaw (placental? mammal), Early Cretaceous (c. 115 million years old), Inverloch, Victoria

Leaellynasaura skull (hypsilophodontid dinosaur), Early Cretaceous (c. 106 million years old), Dinosaur Cove, Victoria

Sciences

Opalised dinosaur femur

Opalised dinosaur bones are unique to Australia. An opalised fossil bone is formed when the bone itself is dissolved and a silica-rich gel invades the space left behind to create a natural cast. Most of these fossils have been found at Lightning Ridge, New South Wales, where this specimen was collected. It is a femur (or thigh bone) of a group of small, kangaroo-like herbivorous dinosaurs known as hypsilophodontids. Because of their durability, femora are the most commonly found bones. At least two hypsilophodontid species based on femora alone are known from Lightning Ridge, while in what was then polar Victoria, six different species, again represented primarily by femora, are known. There is a greater variety of hypsilophodontids in Victoria than anywhere else on Earth. TR

Baragwanathia plant

Baragwanathia longifolia was the most advanced land plant alive when it first appeared in the fossil record 410 million years ago. The earliest member of the club mosses, it had a much more elaborate arrangement of tiny internal tubes (the vascular system) for transporting nutrients and gases than did the much smaller and less advanced contemporaneous land plants found elsewhere. This species is among the oldest vascular land plants. Because of its relatively advanced structure, the exact geological age of this plant has been the subject of controversy ever since the species was first described and named in 1935 by Melbourne palaeobotanist Isabella Cookson, working in association with an English colleague.

While the largest *B. longifolia* was a giant of its time, it was only the size of a bush. But during the Carboniferous period (354–298 million years ago), when the vast coalfields of Europe and North America were formed by the accumulation of plant matter in tropical coal swamps, club mosses the size of trees were common. Today, club mosses are small plants, often hardly noticed in modern floras. TR

Hypsilophodontid (dinosaur) femur, Early Cretaceous (c. 106 million years old), Lightning Ridge, NSW

Baragwanathia longifolia (club moss), Late Silurian (c. 415 million years old), Yarra Track, Victoria

Fossil sea star

This specimen of a fossil sea star, belonging to the species *Eocatis stachi*, was found in 1980 near the corner of Russell and La Trobe streets during excavations for the Melbourne Underground Rail Loop. Numerous other fossil sea stars and other types of echinoderms, such as ophiuroids (brittle stars), crinoids (sea lilies), and extinct groups such as cystoids, edrioasteroids, blastoids, ophiocistioids and the bizarre carpoids, occur in large numbers at certain localities in siltstones and sandstones of Late Silurian and Early Devonian age (400 million to 420 million years ago) in central Victoria. They represent one of the most diverse and scientifically important records of these fossils from rocks of this age. DJH

Trilobite

Trilobites are a group of arthropods that were one of the most abundant types of animals in the oceans between about 540 and 350 million years ago, after which they declined and finally became extinct about 250 million years ago. They are important fossils for dating rocks, interpreting the environments in which the rocks were deposited, and in helping to determine the relative positions of the ancient continents. Trilobites are also popular with fossil collectors because of their great age and their complex and fascinating form. This specimen, of Early Devonian age (approximately 400 million years old), is from Morocco, where many exceptionally well-preserved trilobites have been found. It belongs to the relatively rare genus *Kolihapeltis*, characterised by long, backwardly curving spines arising from above the eyes and the back of the head. DJH

Fossil sea star (*Eoactis stachi*), Late Silurian (c. 420 million years old), Melbourne, Victoria

Trilobite (*Kolihapeltis*), Early Devonian (c. 400 million years old), Morocco

Sciences

Kintore mine minerals

The Kintore open-cut mine is situated along the ridge formed by the outcrop of the Broken Hill ore deposit in western New South Wales. Mines have operated continuously on the deposit since 1883 and have yielded vast amounts of silver, lead and zinc. The primary ore consists of sulphide minerals that contain many different elements. When groundwater containing atmospheric oxygen encounters these minerals they are dissolved, and new secondary minerals crystallise. Many of these are carbonates, phosphates, arsenates and sulphates showing great diversity in chemical composition, colour, crystal size and shape. Many are very rare and a few have never been found elsewhere. With over 300 species recorded there, Broken Hill is one of the world's most mineralogically diverse deposits.

Secondary minerals provide geologists with evidence for chemical processes in the Earth's crust, for example how lead and arsenic are transported in groundwater then locked up by crystals. In order to study these processes, hundreds of rock specimens, encrusted with secondary minerals, were collected in the Kintore open-cut mine during the 1990s. They were sent to the museum for identification and were then added to the mineral collection. The entire suite forms an invaluable scientific record of part of the Broken Hill ore zone, which has now been completely removed by mining. The data have yielded many research papers and a major book that showcases the beauty and diversity of the minerals. BB

1–2

3

1 Chalcophanite crystals with smithsonite on a pillar 3 mm wide, Broken Hill, NSW

2 Olivenite (zincian), 1 mm crystals, Broken Hill, NSW

3 Agardite-(Y), 2 mm crystals, Broken Hill, NSW

George Baker Collection of Tektites

About 770 000 years ago, glassy hailstones pelted down across Australasia. These glassy bodies are called tektites or, locally, australites. It is believed a giant meteorite impacting somewhere in South-East Asia formed them. The impact melted the surrounding Earth rocks, splashing molten material high into the atmosphere and sending some into partial orbit. These glassy rock fragments were then re-melted and aerodynamically sculpted as they passed back through the Earth's atmosphere at high speed, raining down over South-East Asia and Australia. The largest tektites in the field come from Laos, Cambodia, Vietnam and Thailand. Recent studies have postulated a source crater for the tektites in Cambodia although, as yet, no site has been confirmed. One of the best sites for collecting tektites is along the Port Campbell coastline in western Victoria, where the unusual 'button' tektites have been found.

Dr George Baker (1908–75), then of CSIRO in Melbourne, brought the Victorian tektites to international prominence with his pioneering research work. As well as studying tektites, Baker spent much of his holiday time searching for them along the Port Campbell coastline, amassing a collection of more than 3000 specimens. The shape and composition of the button tektites were utilised by NASA during the development of the re-entry vehicles for the Apollo missions in the late 1960s and early 1970s. Baker bequeathed his collection to the museum in 1976. Subsequently, specimens from the collection have helped to resolve issues related to the timing of the impact event that formed the tektites. DAH

1 Typical core and dumbell-shaped tektites from Victoria
2 Perfect button tektites shaped by rapid passage through the Earth's atmosphere, diam. 2.5 cm, Port Campbell, Victoria

Sciences

Cranbourne and Murchison meteorites

In 1854, two large iron meteorites were discovered near Cranbourne, Victoria. In 1860, they were identified as meteoritic, arousing international scientific interest. The Cranbourne No 1 mass, weighing 3500 kilograms, and the Cranbourne No 2, weighing 1525 kilograms, were at that time among the largest known meteorites. The owner of No 1 donated it to 'Mother England', and by purchasing No 2 for £300 in 1862, the British Museum (Natural History), London, acquired both meteorites. Prominent colonial scientists, led by the National Museum director, Frederick McCoy, were outraged at the loss of such important specimens. Through negotiation, and to ease political tensions, the British Museum donated the No 2 mass to the National Museum of Victoria. The No 1 has been exhibited in London since 1865 and remains the centrepiece of that museum's meteorite display.

The rare carbonaceous chondrite meteorite that fell around the township of Murchison in northern Victoria in 1969 has probably been the subject of more scientific publications than any other meteorite. The Murchison meteorite is believed to represent a fragment of cometary material and similarities have been drawn between the compositions of the Murchison meteorite and the Comet Hyakutake. The Murchison meteorite also contains some very old mineral grains, which formed around stars long before the formation of our sun and solar system 4.5 billion years ago. Much research has focused on the wide variety of organic molecules present in the Murchison meteorite, including amino acids – the building blocks of DNA and life. In recent years, structures that could represent primitive life forms, such as bacteria, have been identified. DAH

1 The Cranbourne No 2 mass, 1525 kg. Twelve pieces of the iron meteorite were discovered between 1854 and the early 1930s, in the region spread out along a flight path stretching from Beaconsfield in the north-east to Langwarrin in the south-west.

2 Two large fragments of the Murchison meteorite, 1.1 kg (left) and 1.32 kg (right). The original mass broke up in flight, scattering more than 100 kg of fragments over an area 11 km long by 3.2 km wide. Most fragments weigh less than 200 gm.

Treasures of the Museum

Crystal King

For two years, Alex Amess searched for a clear quartz crystal to facet the world's largest hand-cut stone. In 1971, he selected a 14-kilogram crystal, 25 centimetres high, from the Crystal King Mine near Tallangalook in the Strathbogie Ranges of Victoria, and set about creating the 'Crystal King'. Setting all the facet angles by eye rather than machine was painstaking work, with the cutting and polishing taking 200 hours over three and a half months. The Crystal King has become an icon and inspiration to Australian gem cutters and lapidaries, although it is no longer the world's largest hand-cut stone. DAH

Beryl crystals

During the mid-1980s to the mid-1990s, some spectacular gem minerals were found in remote regions of Pakistan and Afghanistan. The museum acquired many fine specimens for its reference collection, including this spectacular group of gem-quality beryl crystals (variety aquamarine). From the Sumire area, Hunza, Pakistan, the specimen is considered one of the best unearthed during this time. DAH

Crystal King, 8510 carats, 1.7 kg, 19 cm across, 196 facets, Strathbogie Ranges, Victoria

Beryl crystals (aquamarine) with muscovite (brown), 35 cm across, Sumire area, Pakistan

Sciences

E.J. Dunn Collection of Gold and Diamonds

Edward John Dunn (1844–1937) was a noted geologist who explored and collected in Australia and South Africa. Born in Bristol, England, Dunn emigrated to Australia with his family in 1849. His fascination with minerals, especially gold and gemstones, was nurtured during his boyhood in the Victorian goldmining town of Beechworth, where the surrounding mining fields were a rich source of specimens. His collecting continued throughout his adult life as a pioneering geologist, firstly with the Geological Survey of Victoria, then in South Africa between 1871 and 1886. For much of the rest of his life he was based in Victoria, as a consulting geologist and as the director of the Geological Survey from 1904 to 1912. These were times of mineral exploration and mining booms in both countries, and Dunn took advantage of every opportunity to obtain samples during his travels. He donated generously to many museums throughout his life.

There were four major components to his collections that were first offered to the museum in the late 1940s by his surviving family. A suite of 67 South African diamonds, showing a diverse range of colours and forms, was purchased for £125. A gold collection containing 625 specimens, many of which were used to illustrate Dunn's self-published book *The Geology of Gold*, was acquired for £660. His family donated an extensive reference collection of minerals and rocks from mines in Australia and South Africa. Ethnological objects from Australia and the Pacific Islands were also donated. BB

1

2

Gold in iron oxide, 3.7 cm across, Ross Hill, East Transvaal, South Africa
Diamonds, the largest 5.5 mm across, Beechworth district, Victoria

Bunyip gold nugget

Gold nuggets are a feature of the Victorian goldfields, both historically and at present; fossickers with metal detectors are uncovering nuggets missed by the early gold diggers. While the Bunyip nugget, weighing 1.55 kilograms (50 ounces), is only small by Victorian standards, very few of similar dimensions survive in museum collections. The nugget was ploughed up by a farmer near Bridgewater, west of Bendigo. Its location, close to the Loddon River and well away from other nugget finds, suggests the Bunyip nugget might have been carried some distance by Aboriginal people. It was purchased by the National Museum of Victoria in 1978 for $40 000. BB

Bunyip nugget, H 11 cm, Bridgewater district, Victoria

 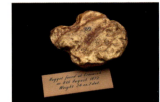

Gold nugget replicas

Victorian gold was characterised by large nuggets. When significant nuggets were discovered during the 19th century, the Department of Mines recorded the information in a catalogue and assembled newspaper reports. More than 1200 nuggets weighing over 620 grams (20 troy ounces) had been found by 1910. The department also made replicas of about 100 large nuggets, based on sketches and photographs. These gold nugget replicas were made from casts using plaster of Paris, and were then painted. The collections of the Geological Survey that were transferred to the museum in 1988 include the nugget replicas and associated information. The museum continues to make replicas of large nuggets found by hobby collectors using metal detectors. BB

The value in pounds sterling given on the label accompanying each nugget is that of about 1900. The largest nugget replica, 'Lady Brassey', is 14 cm across.

Sciences

Extinct species

Museum visitors are often fascinated by displays of extinct animals. With dinosaurs and other prehistoric animals the interest is easy to understand – they look fantastic. But with the obvious exceptions of the Dodo, Thylacine (Tasmanian Tiger), gigantic Stellar's Sea-cow and various moa species, most animals that have become extinct within the last few hundred years are less spectacular – rats, mice, bats, lizards and small birds, for example. Sadly, we tend to appreciate species more when they are gone: the present we take for granted, the future we often ignore and the past we miss.

Generally, if a species has not been observed for more than 50 years it is declared extinct, but there are no hard and fast rules on extinction. On small islands it is easier to determine whether extinction has occurred due to the limited number of places that a species can be found; on continental land masses it is much more difficult. The Night Parrot from Australia had not been reliably seen for more than 80 years, and it was thought to be extinct until one which had recently died was found in 1990. There have been no substantiated sightings since but the Night Parrot is no longer considered extinct.

Some believe extinction is tragic, while others argue that it is a natural process. Species do disappear or change and new species arise. This pattern of extinction and speciation has been a response to changes in habitat and has fuelled subsequent adaptation for millions of years. However, species are now disappearing at an alarming rate because humans are not only changing habitats, but they are taking these habitats away. Not only are we wiping out species but we are also wiping out the opportunity for new species to arise.

There have been claims by some that new DNA-based technologies will be able to reverse extinctions. This is nonsense and gives people false expectations of what is possible. Unless embryos, eggs and sperm or cells from an extinct species are properly frozen and stored, and a very close living relative can act as a surrogate, the species has gone forever. The critical issue is not to lose a species in the first place. Even in-vitro fertilisation techniques pose no real solution to the problem. Such techniques may allow us to breed more individuals in captivity but that treats the symptom not the cause. Species are usually threatened because their habitat is being lost. Breeding more in captivity is not much good if they have nowhere to go.

The demise of Tasmania's last-known Thylacine in 1937 has captured everyone's imagination. We are left with a few images, some film footage and museum specimens. The museum has several individuals in its collection, represented by skins, skeletons and a sub-adult born at the Royal Melbourne Zoological Gardens.

Thylacine (*Thylacinus cynocephalus*)

Southern Gastric Brooding Frog (*Rheobatrachus silus*)

Sciences

The extinct Laughing Owl was once widespread over both of New Zealand's main islands and Stewart Island. It occurred in two subspecies, *Sceloglaux albifacies albifacies* in the south and *S. albifacies rufifacies* in the north. By the 1880s their numbers had been drastically depleted, and the last authentic report of the bird was in 1914. Specimens are rare in museum collections and our sole specimen of this large owl is a nestling. It is the only known nestling and is therefore extremely important to researchers.

The Paradise Parrot was known to European settlers for less than 80 years. These princely birds were never seen in large numbers, and drought and grazing combined to eliminate them in the 1920s. Today, museum specimens are among our few reminders.

The Southern Gastric Brooding Frog, first recognised in 1973, has not been seen in the wild for more than 20 years. Continued efforts to locate the species have been unsuccessful and it is now presumed to be extinct. The two species of this frog – the Southern and Northern Gastric Brooding Frogs – had amazing and unique reproductive habits. After being swallowed by the female, the fertilised eggs hatched and developed in her stomach. The lining of the female's stomach changed during this time and she did not feed. After several weeks, tiny froglets would be regurgitated and the female frog would resume feeding. LC, NWL & DB

1 New Zealand Laughing Owl (*Sceloglaux albifacies*)
2 Paradise Parrot (*Psephotus pulcherrimus*)

Great Elephant Bird egg

The elephant birds were a large, flightless group of birds that evolved in isolation, largely free from predators, on the island of Madagascar. They were ratites, like the Ostrich, Rhea, Emu, Cassowary and Kiwi. Three species of elephant birds are currently recognised: *Aepyornis hildebrandti*, *A. medius* and *A. maximus*. The largest of these, known as the Great Elephant Bird (*A. maximus*), stood three to four metres high and has been estimated to have weighed 450 kilograms. The elephant birds became extinct around 1642 due largely to the introduction of predators such as pigs, which ate the chicks and destroyed eggs, and from hunting pressure by humans.

The egg of the Great Elephant Bird is thought to be the largest known egg in the world, and has a greater volume than eggs of any of the largest of the non-avian dinosaurs. The eggs measured 89 centimetres in the long circumference and 30 centimetres in length, and had a volume equal to nine litres – equivalent to 15 dozen chickens' eggs.

Eggshell fragments of elephant birds are still commonly found in coastal sand dunes of southern Madagascar. Intact eggs are extremely rare. The bones of elephant birds are also sometimes found in coastal peat deposits. The fossil record of the elephant birds is confined to the past 2 million years. The novelist H.G. Wells, who trained as an anatomist, wrote about the elephant bird in a short story titled '*Aepyornis* Island' (1894). The provenance of the Great Elephant Bird's egg at the museum is unknown. RO'B

Egg of the Great Elephant Bird (*Aepyornis maximus*)

Sciences

Cryogenic collection

Advances in molecular biotechnology during the mid-1980s provided new tools for the museum's scientists studying the origins, evolution and conservation of Australia's unique fauna. It was now possible to include information from an animal's DNA – along with more conventional characteristics such as external appearance, skeletal structures and behaviour – to describe species and their relationships. These new techniques revolutionised the science of taxonomy worldwide and led to the establishment of cryogenic collections containing frozen samples of blood, muscle and other tissues to provide a source of genetic material for study.

The museum entered this new era in 1987 with the establishment of its own cryogenic collection. Material from over 1000 different species, including an extensive collection of samples from Australian and New Guinean birds, are currently preserved in sub-zero conditions (-85° Centigrade), making this one of the largest museum-based cryogenic collections in the world. The collection continues to grow through the addition of different types of material such as small vials of blood taken from Australia's endangered Regent Honeyeaters, packets of Superb Lyrebird feathers collected from nests in Victoria's Dandenong Ranges, and hair samples gently plucked from the backs of the tiny Mountain Pygmy Possums from Australia's alpine regions.

The cryogenic collection is proving to be a valuable resource for conservation studies of Australia's rare and threatened animals. Species whose conservation programs have benefited from access to this resource include the Regent Honeyeater, the Christmas Island Hawk-Owl, the Black-eared Miner, the Glossy-Black Cockatoo and the Mountain Pygmy Possum. The value of the cryogenic collection continues to grow. JN

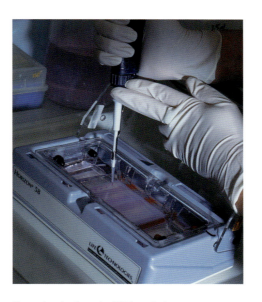

Removing feathers for DNA analysis

The DNA electrophoresis process

Zoological types

The names zoologists use for species of animals become part of the language when they are published in scientific journals, along with a description and identification of a typical specimen or series of specimens – known as 'types'. Among the museum's millions of specimens are several thousand which have this special 'type' status. They are irreplaceable.

Types are necessary to resolve disputes when it is unclear what a name might refer to. This happens if the original published description is inadequate, ambiguous or wrong, or very similar species are recognised at a later time. Contrary to popular opinion, publication of names for newly discovered species is far from over. Previously unnamed species are frequently discovered when taxonomists explore new environments. Or, they realise with the application of molecular methods that what was thought to be one widespread species is more than one. New type specimens are always being added to the museum's collection, which houses types of over 8500 species of invertebrates and almost 500 species of birds, mammals, fish, frogs and reptiles. Each is significant and has its own story.

Leadbeater's Possum was officially introduced to the world as *Gymnobelideus leadbeateri* by Frederick McCoy in 1867. It is restricted to well-forested areas of eastern Victoria. McCoy's original specimens, the types, came from 'scrub on the banks of the Bass River'. McCoy's article was accompanied by excellent line drawings showing detail of the male, its teeth and feet. Today, this possum is considered endangered due to habitat loss.

The first known specimens of the Baw Baw Frog were disgorged by an Eastern Tiger Snake collected in 1898 on Mount Baw Baw, Victoria. Following its initial discovery and subsequent description by Walter Baldwin Spencer in 1901, the Baw Baw Frog was not seen again for over

1

2

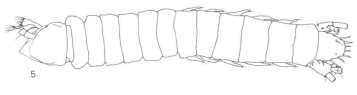

50 years. Now considered critically endangered, the species is restricted to high altitudes on the Mount Baw Baw Plateau.

This Southern Moray was collected by Frederick McCoy in 1884 from Half Moon Bay in Port Phillip Bay. Although there have been many surveys of Port Phillip Bay over the years, his is the only specimen known to exist. It was first thought to be a specimen of the Common Green Moray, but was officially recognised as a new species in 2001.

Yabbies are known to zoologists as *Cherax destructor*, a name proposed in 1936 by E.L. Clark. Her types, over 400 specimens, came from many localities in Victoria and South Australia. Crustacean specialists now believe that this series includes two subtly different species. One individual has been selected as type of the true yabby and another as type of the second species, *C. albidus*.

Most major groups of animals referred to as orders comprise thousands of species; however, one, the bizarre crustacean order Mictacea, has only four. *Hirsutia sandersetalia*, described by Jean Just and Gary Poore in 1988, is an Australian deep-sea species represented by a single damaged type specimen. The only other known specimen of *Hirsutia*, from the deep Atlantic, is in the National Museum of Natural History, Washington.   GP, NWL & DB

1 Holotype of Leadbeater's Possum (*Gymnobelideus leadbeateri*)
2 Baw-Baw Frog (*Philoria frosti*)
3 Southern Moray Eel (*Gymnothorax austrinus*)
4 Part of the type series of the yabby (*Cherax destructor*)
5 Illustration of the holotype of the mictacean crustacean *Hirsutia sandersetalia*, by J. Just & G.C.B. Poore

Treasures of the Museum

William Mountier Bale Collection of Hydroids

Some of the museum's treasures need to be studied through a microscope. The hydroids, marine animals covered with minute polyps, look like tiny feathers attached to the sea floor. Being microscopic and hidden at the bottom of the sea, hydroids did not immediately attract the attention of Australian naturalists in the 19th century.

William Mountier Bale (1851–1940) lived in Kew, Melbourne, and held various positions in the Department of Trade and Customs during his working life. However, his real passion for over 50 years was microscopy and the study of Australian hydroids. He was an active member of the Microscopical Society of Victoria and the Field Naturalists' Club of Victoria in the 1880s and 1890s, joining a group of like-minded gentlemen at monthly meetings to discuss the latest scientific methods and discoveries.

Bale published 13 scientific papers, the most notable being the *Catalogue of the Australian Hydroid Zoophytes* in 1884. He described 126 new hydroid species, and recorded many others from the region for the first time, establishing himself as a world expert on this particular group. Bale worked by mounting specimens of each species on glass slides for study under the microscope, and compiling meticulous descriptions and illustrations from them. His research collection eventually grew to over 1100 microslides, labelled and arranged in systematic order in handsome timber slide cabinets.

In his later years, Bale realised that his collection needed to be safeguarded for the future and he began lodging the most significant parts with the museum. Other material was acquired after his death in 1940. The Bale Collection remains an important foundation in hydroid biology, and an ongoing reference point for marine biologists in Australia and overseas. TS

Microslide cabinet
Original drawing by Bale forms background watermark
Hydroid microslides prepared by Bale

Macpherson, Gabriel and Victorian marine molluscs

Molluscs are among the most attractive groups of marine animals. Their shells come in myriad shapes, textures and colours. The variety includes tiny cowries, ornate muricids, bright volutes and sculptured venerids.

Marine Molluscs of Victoria, published in 1962 by Melbourne University Press in association with the museum, was a landmark study of molluscs in Australia. The book summarised all existing knowledge about every local species, drawing together the descriptions and illustrations for more than 500 species living in Victorian waters. The monograph resulted from collaboration between two museum staff members with decades of expertise between them. Jessica Hope Black (nee Macpherson) (b. 1919) was the National Museum of Victoria's first curator of molluscs from 1946 to 1965. Charles John Gabriel (1879–1963) worked as a pharmacist in Collingwood, but also held the position of honorary curator of molluscs at the museum from 1933 until his death in 1963. The impressive personal collection of shells Gabriel built up over his lifetime was acquired by the museum in 1963, and has become an important cornerstone of the state collection.

The species descriptions in the book were compiled by Macpherson and Gabriel, based on reference specimens in the collection, and accompanied by 486 drawings by George Browning (1918–2000). The artist was a graduate of the National Gallery of Victoria Art School, and was renowned for a series of wildlife dioramas he created for the museum in the 1950s.

For more than 40 years, *Marine Molluscs of Victoria* has been a reference for amateurs and professionals. The book highlights a molluscan fauna found nowhere else in the world, and remains an important record of the biodiversity of the region. TS

Frilled venerid (*Bassina disjecta*)

Sciences

Specimens from the museum's mollusc collection with George Browning's illustrations. From left to right: Long-horned Murex (*Chicoreus damicornis*); Fronded Murex (*Chicoreus denudatus*); Umbilicated Murex (*Muricopsis umbilicatus*); Thorny or Spiny Oyster (*Spondylus tenellus*); Three-shaped Murex (*Pterynotus triformis*)

Port Phillip Bay marine fauna

Port Phillip Bay has always played a significant role in the life of the citizens of Melbourne. It is an access route for shipping, a place for recreation, and it also receives most of the discharge from the city's sewage treatment works. The Port Phillip Biological Survey Committee was established in 1888 to report on the biology of the bay. Collections made then by dredging remain in the museum today. So, too, do more extensive samples taken during the 1950s, 1960s and 1970s by the museum and the Fisheries and Wildlife Department, and the Melbourne and Metropolitan Board of Works, and in the mid-1990s by the museum itself. The first survey was undertaken simply to document the fauna in the new colony, but those taken in the 20th century were concerned about environmental changes resulting from urban and industrial development.

The surveys concentrated on collecting samples of the molluscs, worms, crustaceans and other kinds of animals living in the mud and sand at the bottom of the bay. Thousands of species have been identified over the years, hundreds of them new to science. Together, this series of samples is an historical archive that maps changes in density and distribution of species known to occur in the bay and documents when introduced species have appeared. Interpretation of collections like these inform environmental managers faced with decisions about dealing with waste water in the catchment, the location of marine parks and legislating for fisheries. GP

1–3

4–8

1 Polychaete (*Eupolymnia koorangia*). A burrowing worm

2 Amphipod (*Birubius wirakus*). A species not described until 1978

3 Ghost shrimp (*Biffarius limosus*). One of several new species of burrowing shrimps discovered in the 1970s

4 Heart Urchin (*Echinocardium cordatum*). An abundant burrower in muddy sediments

5 Hydroid (*Clathrozoon wilsoni*). Collected by J.B. Wilson and identified as a new species in 1891

6 Commercial Scallop (*Pecten fumatus*). An edible species that was the basis of a fishery between the 1960s and 1990s

7 Bivalve mollusc (*Theora lubrica*). A dominant species in muddy environments during 1970s, now displaced by another introduced bivalve

8 Sea louse (*Natatolana woodjonesi*). One of many species of scavengers

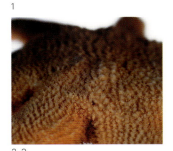

Antarctic zoological collections

The museum has a long association with Antarctica and has built up natural science collections from this continent over almost a century. Examples of penguins, petrels and seals were donated to the museum following the British National Antarctic Expedition of 1901–04, Ernest Shackleton's 1909 exploration and Douglas Mawson's voyages in 1912–14. Among the earliest marine animals collected were protozoans gathered by Shackleton's ship *Nimrod* and ostracod crustaceans dredged by Mawson's ship *Aurora*.

The Australian Antarctic Division was located in Melbourne until 1981, when it moved to Hobart. Most of the biological samples collected by Australian National Antarctic Research Expeditions over the previous 30 or more years have been deposited in the museum. These include a wide variety of marine invertebrates collected from the shores at Antarctic bases Mawson and Davis, and from Macquarie Island and Heard Island in the subantarctic. Museum researchers went to Macquarie Island in 1960 and returned with collections made from intertidal habitats; in 1977 they were involved in the first scuba-diving sampling; and in 1992 they sampled streams on the island. Since 1985, museum marine biologists have participated in many cruises to Antarctica, dredging and trawling around Prydz Bay on the continent and around Heard Island. Extensive collections now housed in the museum are an archive of the animals of the Southern Ocean and complement those held in other museums from other coasts of Antarctica. GP

1 Unicorn Icefish (*Channichthys rhinoceratus*). A fish with no haemoglobin in its blood

2 Sea star (*Solaster subarcuatus*). A predatory sea star from subantarctic islands south of Australia and found also in Bass Strait and around Tasmania

3 Amphipod (*Epimeria similis*). One of numerous species of scavenging amphipod crustaceans in Antarctic waters, and much larger than those found in temperate Australian waters

Deep-sea collections

Ocean covers two-thirds of the surface of the Earth to a depth of four kilometres. It is by far the largest ecosystem. Study of the deep ocean started at the end of the 19th century, though much more recently in Australia. Since the 1980s, marine biologists at the museum have been building collections from the deep sea off the coast of south-eastern Australia to explore the evolutionary history of this extraordinary environment. The sea floor and mid-water have been sampled from oceanographic ships using dredges, trawls and grabs. The continental slope and seamounts are of special interest and have revealed a diverse fauna of fishes, crabs, lobsters, molluscs, corals, sponges and many other things. The museum's deep-sea collections are of global significance because they contain species found nowhere else and are not replicated in other museums.

The most diverse fish family living at or near the deep-sea floor are the grenadiers (family Macrouridae). Although deep-dwelling species are usually thought of as occurring widely in the world oceans, many, like the Faintbanded Whiptail, are confined geographically to areas of coastal continental slopes. The description of this species was based in part on the museum's specimens collected off the southern coast of Australia at depths from 248 to 717 metres.

It is likely that the majority of species in the ocean's deep mid-water produce biological light. Contrary to what might be expected, this assists many to escape notice, helping protect them from becoming a meal for marauding predators. Among the best adapted are the deep-sea hatchetfish, whose downward-directed photophores completely cover the underside of their very compressed bodies. The light they produce matches the dim light coming from above and obscures their profile when seen from below.

Some families of crustaceans, such as polychelid lobsters, are found only in deep, cold water. Polychelids differ from more familiar lobsters in being blind and in having exceptionally long claws. They live on the sea floor, feeding in the dark on small invertebrates they catch with their extended pinchers. At about 15 centimetres long, they are not of commercial interest. About a quarter of the world's 40 species of polychelids occurs in the seas off south-eastern Australia.

Many species of the deep-sea floor have long, thin legs and are larger than their shallow-water cousins. The Giant Sea Spider, with a leg span of 50 centimetres, is an example, adapted to walk gently on the soft mud covering the ocean floor. Sea spiders are only remotely related to more familiar terrestrial spiders. The museum has an important collection of sea spiders from deep-ocean environments, shallower waters and from Antarctica.

Many of the animals found during surveys cannot be identified immediately. These are stored at the museum for specialist taxonomists. Black corals (antipatharians) are tree-like colonies of microscopic animals, like the corals of tropical reefs that are attached to rocky outcrops. Deep-sea corals are poorly understood and the museum's collection will become part of worldwide research in the future. GP & MG

1 New Zealand Hatchetfish (*Polyipnus kiwiensis*)

2 Giant Sea Spider (*Dodecalopoda mawsoni*)

3 Polychelid lobster (*Pentacheles laevis*)

4 Black coral (order Antipatharia)

5 Faintbanded Whiptail (*Caelorinchus amydrozosterus*)

Sciences

1

2

3

4–5

Treasures of the Museum

Exotic species

Through choice and necessity, the first European settlers did not rely on the food sources that had sustained Indigenous Australians for thousands of years; they brought their own crops and stock with them. These animals and plants are now an integral part of our environment – sheep, cattle, horses and wheat on farms, tomatoes, potatoes and beans in our gardens. Decorative species of flowers and trees, and pets as companions added to the list of non-Australian fauna and flora so characteristic of the Australian landscape and cities today. Not all non-Australian species were introduced deliberately; others had unanticipated consequences. The problems caused by the well-intentioned release of rabbits, in 1859, and of blackberries, in 1861, are legend. Lessons learned from the spread of species such as these are responsible for Australia's strict quarantine laws.

The museum's collections are an archive of this changing face of the Australian fauna. Even today, research by museum scientists adds to the catalogue of native fauna, while at the same time newly discovered foreign species continue to be recognised. Early collectors had little interest in acquiring specimens of sparrows, Cabbage Whites or foxes. More recently, however, museum scientists must ask whether a newly found species is foreign or a previously unrecognised native. New discoveries are used to document when the exotics arrived and what environmental impacts they have had.

European settlers soon found Australia's limited freshwater resources boasted few angling species of note. Exceptions such as the Native Grayling, which attracted the attention of colonial anglers, steadily dwindled in numbers with increasing in fishing pressure, and never enjoyed the popularity of angling species such as salmon and trout 'back home'. The first introduced trout finally reached Melbourne alive in April 1864. The offspring from these trout were introduced into Victorian streams, and angling for trout as a recreation commenced. The capture of the first trout, taken from a dam by William Robertson at his Riddells Creek property near Mount Macedon in 1870, was so noteworthy that the fish, which is pictured here, was donated to the museum.

In 1900, a 'Note on the occurrence of the European crab, *Carcinus maenas*, Leach, in Port Phillip' by S.W. Fulton and F.E. Grant was published in the local journal, *Victorian Naturalist*. These authors, who knew the native crabs, sent specimens to crab specialists who all expressed surprise at a European species in Australia when none had been reported in a survey 45 years earlier. The museum still holds these first-collected specimens as well as more recent ones from other localities. The species is very common now and is a serious predator of native shore crabs.

Northern Pacific Sea Star (*Asterias amurensis*)
Brown Trout (*Salmo trutta*)
European Shore Crab (*Carcinus maenas*)
European Wasp (*Vespula germanica*)

Sciences

The Northern Pacific Sea Star is just one of at least 100 exotic marine species in Port Phillip Bay. The large, five-armed sea star is a native of north-western Pacific shores. It was first noticed in Tasmania in 1986, presumably reaching Australia as a hitchhiker in the ballast water of cargo ships. The sea stars remained localised in the Derwent River, Tasmania, until the first individuals were found by scallop fishers in Victoria in 1995. The species is able to reproduce exceptionally rapidly, and now more than 100 million inhabit Port Phillip Bay, where they feed on molluscs and compete with native sea stars.

The European Wasp is one of many exotic species now resident in Australia. It was introduced into Tasmania about 1957, probably from New Zealand where it had become established, and reached mainland Australia in 1977, spreading east along the coast and west to Adelaide. Tracking the actual distribution and predicting the potential spread of the wasp requires specific information such as when it first arrived on mainland Australia. When population modellers make such a predication they set the date for its establishment on mainland Australia by the museum specimen shown here, collected in Melbourne in 1977. GP, MG, KW & TO'H

Treasures of the Museum

Giant Squid

The museum's collection of marine invertebrates (animals without backbones) contains five examples of the biggest invertebrate on Earth: the Giant Squid. These huge, rarely encountered animals can be more than 15 metres long. They live in the dark, cold deep sea in all oceans of the world, including the waters off southern Australia. The museum's specimens were captured between 1996 and 2002 by commercial fishermen in deep-water trawls in Bass Strait, off Portland and off Tasmania. They were caught in depths between 500 and 800 metres.

The Giant Squid is recognised by its two extremely long feeding tentacles, the tips of which bear many sharp-toothed suckers, and its special small suckers with corresponding bumps along the feeding tentacle shafts. The suckers and bumps act like press-studs and allow the tentacles to be zipped together to become one long, snapping claw. Live Giant Squid have never been observed in their natural habitat. Their flesh is full of pockets of ammonia fluid that is lighter than seawater. These fluid pouches cancel out the weight of the muscles and allow the animal to hang in the water without using energy. The Giant Squid probably uses its huge eyes to spot animals that carelessly give off light, and then it attacks with the long feeding tentacles. All around the world, film crews are trying to be the first to film a live Giant Squid in the wild, spending millions of dollars on submarines and special cameras, and even attaching cameras to the heads of sperm whales, hoping the whales will do the filming when they go hunting the squid. MN

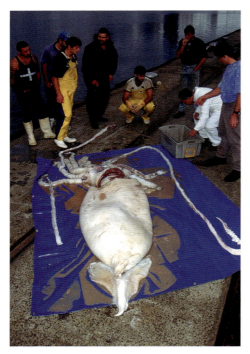

Suckers on the tentacle of a Giant Squid (*Architeuthis sanctipauli*)
Giant Squid on the wharf after being brought to Melbourne on board a fishing boat
Photographer: David Paul, University of Melbourne

Sciences

Blue Whale

In 1867, a 27.5-metre whale was recovered from Jan Juc beach in Victoria and was identified as a Black Right Whale. For many years, the articulated skeleton was displayed outside the museum's building at the University of Melbourne. Due to the ravages of nature, only a few odd bones and some baleen remain, but these are enough to reveal that the individual is in fact Blue Whale. Over the past 100 years, other Blue Whales have been stranded along the Victorian coastline.

Blue Whales are the largest animals ever to live, and they can occasionally be seen in Victoria's deep offshore waters. The skeleton pictured here is of a juvenile male stranded on a beach at Cathedral Rock, near Lorne, Victoria, on 5 May 1992. It weighed 40 tonnes and was 18.7 metres long; removing it from its beached position to the museum required several cranes, a bulldozer and a low loader.

The taxonomy of Blue Whales remains debatable. This specimen has been assigned to the subspecies known as the Pygmy Blue Whale, *Balaenoptera musculus brevicauda*. Many scientists argue that this taxon is merely a subspecies, while others insist it is a separate species. Analysis of DNA might provide further evidence one way or the other.

Meanwhile, the Blue Whale's articulated skeleton draws an appreciative crowd at the museum. It is by far the largest animal displayed at the museum and epitomises the variety of remarkable fauna found in Victoria. NWL

Blue Whale (*Balaenoptera musculus*)

Treasures of the Museum

Grey Nurse Shark

This magnificent set of jaws from the museum's collection is testament to the presence of the Grey Nurse Shark in Port Phillip Bay during the late 19th century. In his *Prodromus of the Zoology of Victoria*, Frederick McCoy refers to them as being 'one of the largest and most ferocious of our Sharks, and so common as to be an object of great terror to bathers, who occasionally suffer grievous lacerations when caught swimming even near shore'. McCoy goes on to state that the 'Enormous jaws of this species may often be seen in the fishermen's huts along the shore from Picnic Point to Mordialloc'.

The Grey Nurse Shark is all but absent from Victorian waters nowadays, and the species is protected in many parts of Australia. Perhaps their demise was hastened during McCoy's time. The government of the day, concerned about 'the great quantity of fish fit for the table devoured by this species', offered a reward to fishermen based on the length of each Grey Nurse Shark killed. DB

Reticulated Pythons

Originally from Singapore, these two Reticulated Pythons were presented to the museum in 1905 by Paul Ponsole of Fitzgerald Brothers' Circus. The specimens were on display for many years in the McCoy Hall at the museum's Swanston Street location.

Reticulated Pythons grow to become the longest snakes in the world – some individuals reach 10 metres in length. They live near water among rainforests and woodlands throughout much of South-East Asia. They are active at night, and large Reticulated Pythons typically feed on a variety of birds and mammals, including wild pigs, monkeys and small deer. These are not venomous snakes; they kill their prey by squeezing it with their muscular body coils. DB

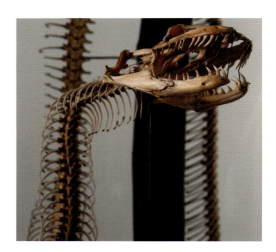

Jaws of the Grey Nurse Shark (*Carcharias taurus*)

Reticulated Pythons (*Python reticulatus*)

Sciences

Chinese butterfly

This butterfly, collected in China in 1742, is the oldest known insect specimen in Australia. It is unclear how the specimen came to be part of the museum collection, though the museum's first director, Frederick McCoy, who purchased many valuable natural history collections, possibly acquired it.

Much can be learnt from this specimen. Its age, more than 260 years, indicates the longevity of cared-for natural history collections. Because the collector recorded a location and a date, the specimen is scientifically useful in providing a biological snapshot from that year. KW

Evening Brown butterfly (*Melanitis leda*)

Hummingbird case

Between 1858 and 1869 the museum purchased 4000 birds from English ornithologist and natural history dealer John Gould. Among these specimens were examples of hummingbirds, of which 328 species are known from the Americas. The museum was keen to display the brilliant colours, shapes and sizes of these foreign birds. The study-skins received from Gould were prepared as mounts by museum taxidermists and displayed attached to open branches so that the iridescence of the feathers was highlighted. This elegant case contains examples of 203 species of hummingbirds. RO'B

Hummingbird case, H 220 x W 89 x D 89

Treasures of the Museum

Western Lowland Gorillas

On 20 June 1865, the museum registered three Western Lowland Gorillas that had been collected by and purchased from M. du Chaillu's expedition into equatorial western Africa. Du Chaillu had ventured into Africa's tropics in search of gorillas and had obtained a number of them. His specimens had been sent to London for preparation. From that collection, Frederick McCoy obtained one adult male, one adult female and one unsexed young.

The museum's original register entry states that these are 'Savage' gorillas; this does not reflect any aggressiveness of the species, rather it implies that the original material was first brought to our knowledge by the American Dr Savage and exhibited by him in 1847.

McCoy's purchase of the gorillas was fortuitous, coming soon after the publication of Charles Darwin's *On the Origin of Species*, which gave rise to the idea that humans and apes shared a common ancestry. Darwin's theory was hotly debated, and Du Chaillu's gorillas were both a catalyst for this debate in Melbourne and a great crowd pleaser. The gorillas remained on continuous exhibition for more than 100 years.

Today, gorillas are totally protected and are listed by the Convention on International Trade in Endangered Species of Wild Fauna and Flora. NWL

Western Lowland Gorillas (*Gorilla gorilla*)

Sciences

Okapi

The Okapi was discovered in 1900 in the Congolese rainforests. The museum received this adult male on 20 January 1916 from Dr Christy who had purchased it from the distinguished taxidermists E. Gerrard and Sons of London.

Originating in the Ituri Forest of the Congo Free State (now the Democratic Republic of Congo) the specimen had made its long journey to Australia via Britain. While the Okapi is now endemic to the Democratic Republic of Congo, it has been suggested the animal also formerly occurred in neighbouring Uganda.

The Okapi's closest relative is the giraffe, although its striped hindquarters and shape would indicate otherwise. Like the giraffe the Okapi has a long, prehensile tongue. The Okapi weighs a third as much as a giraffe, and stands only slightly over a third of its height. As the Okapi is a browser at the edge of the rainforest, it does not need the long neck of a savannah animal.

Today, while the Okapi is not listed as a threatened species, it is protected in the Democratic Republic of Congo. Its numbers are estimated to be in the tens of thousands. Habitat removal would be the main concern for its continued existence. The museum's single mount is believed to be the only Australian example. NWL

Okapi (*Okapia johnstoni*)

Treasures of the Museum

1–5

19th-century medicine chest

This wooden medicine chest from the mid to late 19th century has compartments containing a range of pharmaceuticals. It has been suggested that the chest was used at sea and might have belonged to a sea captain or a ship's surgeon. It provides insight into 19th-century medical and pharmaceutical practices of the time, as well as the type of medical services provided during sea travel.

Many of these pharmaceuticals are long gone from contemporary medicine. Bitter Apple was administered as a purgative for constipation. Dover's Powder, which contained opium and was used as a hypnotic sedative, was once grown on the cliffs of Dover in England. The red resin called Dragon's Blood was useful in the treatment of syphilis. Cocaine, a powerful local anaesthetic, was used in the extraction of teeth. James's Fever Powder contained an irritant, antimony, which induced sweating when applied to the skin. It was believed that sweating alleviated a fever. Chloral could send a patient into a deep sleep. A yellow compound with a penetrating odour, Iodoform acted as an antiseptic when applied to wounds, and was especially useful in the treatment of syphilitic ulcers. Logwood relieved the chronic diarrhoea that was suffered by those with dysentery. A case of pinworms was often remedied with a dose of Worm Powder followed up with castor oil. Rochelle Salts was a saline purgative used for digestive discomfort and the relief of constipation. An astringent made from plants and appropriately titled Pile Ointment was used in the treatment of haemorrhoids. NV

6

1 Medicine chest (19th century), H 42 x W 62 x D 38 cm
2 Cocaine
3 Dover's Powder
4 James's Fever Powder
5 Chloral
6 Dragon's Blood

Sciences

Early medical products from the Commonwealth Serum Laboratories

The Commonwealth Serum Laboratories (CSL) was founded in 1916 to provide life-saving products to a country isolated by war. The organisation is renowned for its work in the areas of penicillin, antivenoms, hormones, vaccines and blood products. In 1994, CSL Ltd was listed on the Australian Stock Exchange and has achieved considerable success in the international market for bioproducts. The museum's CSL collection covers the period from 1916 to 1984. The objects were originally collected by CSL staff and volunteers for the CSL Museum, which was once located at the CSL site at Parkville. The displayed objects highlight some of the contributions made by CSL to public health.

The first vaccine produced by CSL in 1919 was used to protect Australians from the pandemic of Spanish influenza.

By the 1930s, CSL was producing a variety of products. CSL's first medical sales representative used this case, containing 65 samples, while travelling the east coast of Australia. Products included insulin and vaccines to diphtheria, gonorrhoea and typhoid.

CSL is renowned for having rapidly implemented methods for the large-scale manufacture of penicillin following the discoveries of Howard Florey in 1939. By 1944, penicillin was available to Australians fighting in the Pacific. Australian citizens were the first in the world to have general access to penicillin.

In 1930, CSL and the Walter and Eliza Hall Institute developed the first antivenom to a bite from a tiger snake. CSL continued to develop antivenoms to all venomous Australian snakes, as well as the Red-back Spider and Funnel-web Spider. NV

CSL tiger snake antivenom (1959)

CSL medical specimen case (c. 1930), H 11 x W 55 x D 43 cm

Early samples of CSL penicillin (1944) and its vaccine to Spanish influenza (1919)

A selection of medical instruments used by Weary Dunlop following the Second World War:

1 Rigid cystoscope (c. 1950). Used to examine the bladder

2 Dr H. von Recklinghauser sphygmomanometer in its original Bakelite case (c. 1940). Used for measuring blood pressure

3 Humby skin-grafting knife (c. 1950). Used to remove large sections of skin for grafting

4 Custom-made gallstone scoop and hook (c. 1950). Used to remove gallstones from a gallbladder during surgery

5 Tonsil guillotine (c. 1950). Used for performing tonsillectomies

Sir Zelman Cowen

The medical instruments of a truly great Australian

Sir Edward Dunlop (1907–93) was a truly great Australian. His fellow medical students at the University of Melbourne gave him the nickname 'Weary', which remained with him throughout his life. He was anything but that; a tall, robust man, he was a heavyweight boxing champion and represented Australia in rugby union. Sporting prowess was matched with outstanding success in his studies: he graduated with first-class honours in medicine and surgery.

At the outbreak of the Second World War, he was a surgeon at St Mary's Hospital, London. He promptly enlisted in the Australian Sixth Division, and served in the Middle East, Greece, Crete and Tobruk. When war came with Japan, his medical unit was sent to Java, where he had command of a hospital in Bandung. When Java fell to the Japanese, he became a prisoner of war. In 1943, Australian prisoners of war under Dunlop's command were sent to work on the Burma–Thailand Railway, and he remained at this infamous location until the end of the war. In appalling conditions, Dunlop and other doctors, including Albert Coates, worked ceaselessly to save men who were frequently suffering from diseases such as malaria, dysentery and cholera, aggravated by chronic malnourishment and, often, by torture.

Weary Dunlop displayed outstanding courage and capacity for leadership. He opposed attempts by the Japanese to compel sick men to work, and for this he was subjected to severe beatings. He showed extraordinary surgical skill and saved many lives. Twice he came very close to death by execution. He kept a detailed diary, published in 1986, which is a compelling tale of pain and endurance told with singular calm and clarity. I cherish the signed copy that was given to my wife and me.

After the war, the importance of a close association with Asia was a continuing theme in Dunlop's life. On the Burma Railway, he had sometimes treated Japanese soldiers, and he became aware, as he put it, 'of the Buddhist belief that all men are equal in the face of death'. He made several visits to Japan, and expressed the hope that 'some increased understanding should emerge from a tragic conflict in which, when all is said and done, Japanese losses vastly exceeded our own'.

His associations with Asia, including participation in the Colombo Plan, and his work in Thailand, Sri Lanka and India, and as team leader of the Australian surgical team working for the civilian population of South Vietnam, left him 'with the conviction that all the races of mankind bear some special mark of God's tenderness, some unique contribution to human kind'.

On Anzac Day 1994, Weary Dunlop's ashes were scattered over the Burma Railway by Prime Minister Paul Keating.

The Rt Hon. Sir Zelman Cowen, AK, GCMG, GCVO, QC, DCL, is the former Governor-General of Australia.

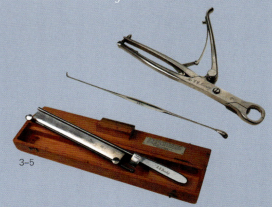

3–5

Notes on Contributors

Phillip Adams, AO, has been a newspaper columnist for half a century. His radio program, *Late Night Live*, is broadcast on Radio National and Radio Australia.

Stephanie Alexander is a food writer and a partner in Richmond Hill Cafe & Larder. Her fifth book, *The Cook's Companion*, is regarded a kitchen bible.

Lindy Allen is Senior Curator of Northern Australia, Indigenous Cultures Department, Museum Victoria.

Dr Philip Batty is Senior Curator of Central Australia, Indigenous Cultures Department, Museum Victoria.

Dr Bill Birch is Senior Curator of Geology, Sciences Department, Museum Victoria.

Dianne J. Bray is Collection Manager of Ichthyology & Herpetology, Sciences Department, Museum Victoria.

Martin Bush is Curator of Earth and Space, Sciences Department, Museum Victoria.

Eddie Butler-Bowdon, formerly Senior Curator in the Australian Society and Technology Department, is Program Manager of Art & Heritage Collections, Melbourne City.

Margaret Cameron, AM, D.Univ, was a member of the council of the museum from 1987 to 1996. She is a fellow of the Royal Australasian Ornithologists Union.

Dr Les Christidis is Head of the Sciences Department, Museum Victoria.

Matthew Churchward is Senior Curator of Technology & Innovation, Australian Society and Technology Department, Museum Victoria.

Sir Zelman Cowen, AK, GCMG, GCVO, QC, DCL, is the former Governor-General of Australia.

Carol Cooper is Manager of Registration at the National Museum of Australia, Canberra, and the current president of the Australian Registrars Committee.

Liza Dale-Hallett is Senior Curator of Technology & Sustainable Futures, Australian Society and Technology Department, Museum Victoria.

David Demant is Curator of Information Technology, Australian Society and Technology Department, Museum Victoria.

Dr David Dorward is Director of the African Research Institute, LaTrobe University, Melbourne.

Penny Edmonds, formerly Curator in the Indigenous Cultures Department, is currently undertaking a PhD in the History Department at the University of Melbourne.

Gary Foley is Senior Curator of South-eastern Australia, Indigenous Cultures Department, Museum Victoria.

Dr Richard Gillespie is Head of the Australian Society and Technology Department, Museum Victoria.

Dr Martin F. Gomon is Senior Curator of Ichthyology, Sciences Department, Museum Victoria.

Dr J. Patrick Greene is Chief Executive Officer of Museum Victoria.

Dermot A. Henry is Senior Collection Manager Sciences Department, Museum Victoria.

Dr Robin Hirst is Director of Collections, Research & Exhibitions, Museum Victoria.

Dr David J. Holloway is Senior Curator of Invertebrate Palaeontology, Sciences Department, Museum Victoria.

Dr Colin Hope is Director of the Centre for Archaeology and Ancient History, Monash University, and a research associate of Museum Victoria, where he was Curator of Mediterranean Antiquities for several years.

John Kean is Exhibition Producer, Exhibitions Planning & Coordination Department, Museum Victoria.

Fiona Kinsey is Curator of Social & Domestic Life, Australian Society and Technology Department, Museum Victoria.

John Landy is Governor of Victoria.

N.W. Longmore is Collection Manager of Ornithology & Mammalogy, Sciences Department, Museum Victoria.

Maryanne McCubbin is Head of Strategic Collection & Information Management, Museum Victoria.

Moya McFadzean is Senior Curator of Immigration & Cultural Diversity, Australian Society and Technology Department, Museum Victoria.

Anne Miller is a volunteer guide for Museum Victoria.

Dr Janette Norman is Senior Curator of Molecular Biology, Sciences Department, Museum Victoria.

Dr Mark Norman is Senior Curator of Molluscs, Sciences Department, Museum Victoria.

Rory O'Brien is Assistant Collection Manager of Ornithology & Mammalogy, Sciences Department, Museum Victoria.

Dr Tim O'Hara is Senior Curator of Marine Invertebrates, Sciences Department, Museum Victoria.

Louise Partos, former Producer in Bunjilaka and Project Coordinator in the Indigenous Cultures Department, is Manager of Bula'bula Arts, Ramingining, Central Arnhem Land.

Dr Gary Poore is Senior Curator of Crustacea, Sciences Department, Museum Victoria.

Alison Raaymakers is Assistant Collection Manager, Australian Society and Technology Department, Museum Victoria.

Michael Reason is Assistant Curator, Australian Society and Technology Department, Museum Victoria.

Dr Thomas H. Rich is Senior Curator of Vertebrate Palaeontology, Sciences Department, Museum Victoria.

Dr Gaye Sculthorpe, formerly Head of the Indigenous Cultures Department, is a member of the National Native Title Tribunal.

Tim Stranks is Project Officer, Collections, Research & Exhibitions Division, Museum Victoria.

Maria Tence is Manager of Public Programs, Immigration Museum, Museum Victoria.

Benjamin Thomas is a doctoral student at the University of Melbourne. He produced both his honours and Masters theses on Museum Victoria's arms collection.

Dr Ron Vanderwal is Senior Curator of Oceania, Indigenous Cultures Department, Museum Victoria.

Dr Nurin Veis is Senior Curator of Human Biology & Medicine, Sciences Department, Museum Victoria.

Dr Ken Walker is Senior Curator of Entomology, Sciences Department, Museum Victoria.

Robyn Williams is a broadcast journalist and science writer. He presents *The Science Show* each week on ABC Radio National and is a fellow of the Australian Academy of Science.

Elizabeth Willis is Senior Curator of Public & Institutional Life, Australian Society and Technology Department, Museum Victoria.

Acknowledgments

A tremendous number of people have contributed to *Treasures of the Museum*. Museum Victoria would like to thank the writers and photographers for illuminating so superbly the highlights the collection. This would have been impossible without the effort of an expert team of conservators, collection managers and assistants, and exhibitions collections coordinators.

Many individuals in the Production Studio deserve thanks for their part in producing the book, most notably the image and copyright managers, digital production officers and book designers. Thanks also to freelance editor Bryony Cosgrove for her work on the text.

Museum Victoria would like to acknowledge the Victorian state government for its support of this publication.

Photography credits

Jon Augier: pages 13, 25, 27, 42, 52, 53 (time ball), 56, 62, 68, 69, 70 (bikes), 73, 74, 75 (printing press), 124 (mask)

John Broomfield: pages x, 6 (Museum Victoria and the Royal Exhibition Building), 10 (pistol), 19 (tomatoes), 59 (safety hood), 60, 67, 75 (statue), 86 (apron), 90 (mat), 92, 98 (carving), 119 (carved tuna), 120–1, 162 (flea)

Frank Coffa: pages 7 (Royal Exhibition Building), 169, 172, 173, 174 (Bunyip nugget), 162 (fish, feather)

Benjamin Healley: pages 10 (Flintlock blunderbuss, matchlock musket), 11, 16, 17, 18 (stove), 20, 29, 32, 39, 44, 53 (clock), 54, 55 (sledge, mask, snow shoe, piano accordion), 57, 58 (plough), 64, 71, 85, 115 (bowls), 123, 126, 127, 128, 129, 130, 131, 132, 134 (birch bark box), 135, 137, 150, 152, 153 (cowry), 157 (cabinet),165

(*Zygomaturus*), 175, 176, 179 (electrophoresis), 180 (frog), 181 (eel, yabbies), 186 (hydroid, scallop, bivalve mollusc), 187 (sea star, amphipod), 189 (New Zealand Hatchetfish, black coral, Faintbanded Whiptail), 190 (sea star), 191 (crabs), 192 (tentacle), 194, 196, 197, 198

Michelle McFarlane: pages 14, 15, 10 (mechanical bank), 19 (lemon, orange, pears, cherries, plum, apple), 24, 30–1, 33, 46–7, 48, 55 (barometer, thermometers), 58 (barbed wire), 63, 70 (medals, trophies), 72, 90 (eel trap), 93 (blanket), 94 (container), 95, 98 (*tanga*), 112, 113, 114, 115, 122, 133, 134 (feather box), 138 (mummified head, coffin), 142, 144, 146, 147, 149, 153 (shark), 154, 155, 156, 157 (eggs), 170, 174 gold replicas), 177, 179 (feather analysis), 180 (possum), 187 (Unicorn Icefish), 190 (Brown Trout), 195, 199, 200–1

Michael Marmach: page 186 (burrowing worm, amphipod, ghost shrimp, Heart Urchin, sea louse)

Mark Norman: page 189 (polychelid lobster, Giant Sea Spider)

Rodney Start: pages 21, 46–7, 59 (steam traction engine), 80–1, 82, 83, 88, 96–7, 107, 109, 110 (axes and picks), 111, 138 (sarcophagus), 145, 146, 154 (Mulgara), 160, 161, 163, 164,165 (*Diprotodon*), 166, 167, 168, 171, 178, 182–3, 184–5, 191 (wasp), 193

Index

altazimuth 56
amphipod 186, 187
ancestral figure 125, 126
Antarctic collections 55, 187
antivenom 199
apron, fibre 86
Arrernte Women … 118
Atininga Avenging Party … 118
Australian Children's Folklore Collection 15
autograph book 15
bags, pandanus and sedge 95
Baker, G., Collection of Tektites 170
Bale, W.M., Collection of Hydroids 182–3
banner
    Ancient Order of Forresters' 49
    eight-hour day 45
baragwanathia plant 167
barbed wire 58
bark cloth 124
bark painting
    Jilamara 100
    Mildjingi 102
    Murayana 100
    Nygalyod devours … 101
    Tjapu 103
    Yungwalia 102
barometer 55
basket
    bicornial 94
    Tasmanian 86
Baw Baw Frog 180–1
beryl crystals 172
bicycles 70–1
Biggest Family Album 38
black box 72
Blandowski, William 147–9
blanket, rainforest 93
blizzard mask 55
Blue Whale 193
body armour 122
body ornaments 113
boomerang 106–7
box
    birch bark 134
    feather 134
    Le Souëf 88
boxing gown 92
boxing truck, Harry Johns 74
Bramble Shark 152–3
Brown Trout 190–1
Bungaleen's grave marker 83
Bunyip gold nugget 174
Burston, George 71

cable, telegraph 25
cable tram 64
camera, Sutton panoramic 27
canoe
    bark, Wurandjeri 85
    Solomon Islands 120–1
caravan 69
carousel, model 16–17
carved human figure 84
Cerebus 11
Charlotte Dundas, model and drawings 66–7
Chinese butterfly 195
Chisholm, Caroline 34–5
cloak
    feather 133
    possum-skin 82
club 123
coach, Concord 68
coffin, Tamenkhamun 138–9
coherer 25
coins 21, 46–7
Coles Book Arcade 62
Commonwealth Serum Laboratories 199
container, decorated 94
Cotton, John 158–9
countermarch loom 39
Cranbourne meteorite 171
Cryogenic collection 179
Crystal King 172
CSIRAC 28–9
Cudmore, F.A., Collection of Tertiary Fossils 163
Curtis, F., Collection of Insects 161
cystoscope 200–1
Darwin, Charles 146
Dawn of Art, The 104–5
deep-sea collections 188–9
Deliverette 73
Descriptive Chart of Common Insectivorous
    Birds … 158–9
diamonds 173
dinosaurs, Victorian 166
Diprotodon 165
Duckmanton, Eliza 22–3
Duigan biplane 72
Dunlop, Edward 'Weary' 200–1
Dunn, E.J., Collection of Gold and Diamonds 173
Dusky Lory 144–5
ECT machine 48
eel trap, woven 90
egg
    Giant Elephant Bird 178
    Australian Magpie 157
Egyptian antiquities 138–9

European Shore Crab 190–1
European Wasp 190–1
exotic species 190–1
extinct species 175–7
Faintbanded Whiptail 188–9
femur, opalised 167
fertility figure 137
Flintlock blunderbuss 10
flute stopper 127
forehead ornaments 113
fossil mammals, Victorian 166
fossils 162–8
gallstone scoop and hook 200–1
ghost shrimp 186
giant fossil cowry 151–3
Giant Gippsland Earthworm 150–1
Giant Sea Spider 188–9
Giant Squid 192
glass points, Kimberley 109
gold 173–4
gold replicas 174
Gould, John 142–3
graptolites 164
Great Pampa-Finch 146
Greek shadow puppets 30–1
Grey Nurse Shark 194
Haasts Bluff 99
Halley, J.J. 158–9
headdress
    ceremonial 115, 127
    mourning 114
Heart Urchin 186
Hirsutia 181
Holmes, D., Collection of Butterflies
    and Moths 160
honour certificate 12
house ornament 130
Howard, Dorothy 15
Howitt, Alfred William 156
hummingbird case 195
hydroid 186
hydroid microslide 182–3
immigration 30–1
Indian matchlock musket 10
irawaki figure 132
Jilamara 100
kente cloth 136
Kintore minerals 169
knives and sheaths 111
knucklebones 15
Koonwarra fossil bed 162
Le Forgeron Marionettes 63
Leadbeater's Possum 180

205

letter 32
Lionel Rose 92
Little Lon 21
'Little Men' 62
machine gun, Nordenfelt 11
mandolin 33
manuscript, John Cotton 158–9
marine fauna, Port Phillip Bay 186
marine molluscs, Victorian 184–5
mask
    courting 128
    crocodile 124
    didagur 132
mass measures 52
Massacre and Rover Thomas Story ... 108
mat, woven 90
matchbook album 24
Max Mints toys 14
McCoy, Frederick 2–3, 150–3
mechanical bank, Punch and Judy 18
medals 46–7, 70
medicine chest, 19th-century 198
micro-ruling engine 52
microslide cabinet 182
mimih figures 96–7
minerals 169–74
mining model, Clunes 44
models 16–17, 25, 42, 44, 58
molluscs, Victorian 184–5, 186
Monograph of the Psittacidae ... 158–9
morse system 25
moths 160
mug, Little Lon 21
Mulgara 154
mummified head 138–9
mummy, Tjeby 138–9
Murchison meteorite 171
Murray Spiny Crayfish 151–2
neck ornament 113
needle telegraph 25
New Zealand Hatchetfish 188–9
New Zealand Laughing Owl 177
Ngalyod Devours a Hunter 101
Northern Hopping Mouse 155
Northern Pacific Sea Star 190–1
Northern Quoll 155
Numismatic Collection, The 46–7
Okapi 197
Opening of the First Federal Parliament ... 51
Opperman, Hubert 70
orator's stool 129
orrery 13

paddle-steamer engine 42
Paradise Parrot 177
pearl-shell ornaments 112
pencil sketch, Wurundjeri 78
penicillin samples 199
Phar Lap 1, 60–1
photograph album covers 33
photograph album, Charles Walter 87
piano accordion 55
Pig-footed Bandicoot 147, 149
Pintupi Man with a Lizard, Shield & Spear 117
Pintupi Men Drinking from a Desert Lake 116
pipe, Little Lon 21
pistol, Savage No 1 10
polychaete 186
polychelid lobster 188–9
pot lid (hair oil), Little Lon 21
printing press, Fawkner 75
proclamation board 89
projector, triunial 27
psychiatric items 48
puppets 30–1, 63
rambaramp 131
recipe and remedy book 22–3
Red Bird-of-Paradise 145
regulator clock 53
Reticulated Pythons 194
rigar kore 136
rotative beam engine 42
Rough Knob-tailed Gecko 155
Royal Exhibition Building 50
Rutherglen Corroboree 79
safety hood, PMA 59
saucer, Little Lon 21
scrapbook, Caroline Chisholm 34–5
sea louse 186
sea star 168, 187
shell-inlay objects 119
shield
    rainforest 93
    south-eastern 80–1
Silver Perch 147–8
skin-grafting knife 200–1
sledge 54, 55
slingshot 15
snow shoe 55
snuff box 11
Southern Cassowary 143
Southern Gastric Brooding Frog 176–7
Southern Moray Eel 181
Southern Mountain Cavy 146
spearthrower 110

specimen case 199
Spencer, Walter Baldwin 2, 154
sphygmomanometer 200–1
Spinifex Hopping Mouse 154
spirit figure 126
Spotswood Pumping Station 43
stained-glass window 36–7
standard yard measure 52
Standardwing 142–3
statue, *Mercury* 75
steam car 65
steam traction engine 16–17, 59
Stick-nest Rat 147, 149
stone axes and picks 110
stove 18
straightjacket 48
stump jump plough 58
suitcase 32
Sulphur-crested Cockatoo 158–9
Sunshine Stripper Harvester 57
survey post 56
symphonion 62
tanga 98
tektites 170
telephone, double-pole magneto 26
textiles, African 136
thermometers 55
Thomson, Donald 1–2, 155
Thylacine 175
Tiwi pole 98
tonsil guillotine 200–1
totem pole 135
trade literature 40–1
trilobite 168
Trout Cod 147–8
types, zoological 180–1
Unicorn Icefish 187
vaccine, Spanish influenza 199
Wallace, Alfred 144–5
washing machines 20
wasps 161
wax fruit and vegetables 19
wedding cape 123
Western Lowland Gorillas 196
White, H.L., Collection of Australian
    Birds' Eggs 157
White-footed Rabbit Rat 156
White-winged Fairy-wren 156
working models case 42
Wurreka 91
yabbies 181
Zygomaturus 165